THE
ANXIETY HEALER'S GUIDE

THE
ANXIETY
HEALER'S
GUIDE

Coping Strategies *and* Mindfulness Techniques
to Calm *the* Mind *and* Body

Alison Seponara, MS, LPC

SIMON ELEMENT

New York   London   Toronto   Sydney   New Delhi

SIMON
ELEMENT

An Imprint of Simon & Schuster, Inc.
1230 Avenue of the Americas
New York, NY 10020

First Simon Element hardcover edition March 2022

SIMON ELEMENT is a trademark of Simon & Schuster, Inc.

For information about special discounts for bulk purchases, please contact Simon & Schuster Special Sales at 1-866-506-1949 or business@simonandschuster.com.

The Simon & Schuster Speakers Bureau can bring authors to your live event. For more information or to book an event, contact the Simon & Schuster Speakers Bureau at 1-866-248-3049 or visit our website at www.simonspeakers.com.

Interior design by Jennifer Chung

Manufactured in the United States of America

1   3   5   7   9   10   8   6   4   2

Library of Congress Cataloging-in-Publication Data

Names: Seponara, Alison, author.
Title: The anxiety healer's guide : coping strategies and mindfulness techniques to calm the mind and body / by Alison Seponara, MS, LPC. Description: First Simon Element hardcover edition. | New York : Simon Element, 2022. | Includes bibliographical references. Identifiers: LCCN 2021030890 (print) | LCCN 2021030891 (ebook) | ISBN 9781982177829 (hardcover) | ISBN 9781982177836 (ebook) Subjects: LCSH: Anxiety. | Mindfulness (Psychology) | Mind and body. Classification: LCC BF575.A6 S473 2022 (print) | LCC BF575.A6 (ebook) | DDC 152.4/6—dc23
LC record available at https://lccn.loc.gov/2021030890
LC ebook record available at https://lccn.loc.gov/2021030891

ISBN 978-1-9821-7782-9
ISBN 978-1-9821-7783-6 (ebook)

Illustration Credits: Hand by Adrien Coquet from the Noun Project. Heart, Labyrinths, and Mazes by Alexander Skowalsky from the Noun Project. Moon by angelina from the Noun Project. Walk by Bakunetsu Kaito from the Noun Project. Emoticon by Caesar Rizky Kurniawan from the Noun Project. Brain by Cédric Villain from the Noun Project. Sun by gufron m from the Noun Project. Person by Guilherme Furtado from the Noun Project. Abstract Flower and Flower by Hassan Khaled from the Noun Project. Floral, Flower, and Leaves by Kristina Margaryan from the Noun Project. Stop Sign by Libby Ventura from the Noun Project. Star by M. Oki Orlando from the Noun Project. Mandala by Maria Zamchy from the Noun Project. Butterfly by Oliver Kittler from the Noun Project. Sun by Pixel Bazaar from the Noun Project. Leaf by PJ Souders from the Noun Project. Flower by Xinh Studio from the Noun Project.

For Mila and Paolo
Who always remind me that laughter is the best medicine . . .
and my reasons for healing

And because of Mom, Dad, Amy, and Jonny
Thank you for always accepting me,
loving me, and believing in me . . .
anxiety and all . . .

Contents

Introduction

Welcome to *The Anxiety Healer's Guide*! I am so grateful to be on this journey with you not only as a therapist but also as a fellow healer recovering from anxiety myself. As someone who has always struggled with anxiety (and made a career out of learning how to ease it), I am constantly looking for ways to help calm my overactive mind and body when faced with adversity. I was the little girl with stomachaches who never wanted to sleep over at her friend's house. The teenager who never felt good enough. The college girl who always felt like she was "dying" and lived at the doctor's office. The adult who was expected to be the life of the party but in reality struggled with severe social anxiety. I began making choices based on what others expected of me and felt pressure to be someone I wasn't. I felt a constant need to be perfect and not "rock the boat" by talking about my feelings. When I tried to openly express feelings of sadness, worry, or anger, I was constantly dismissed with the phrase "oh, you're fine." I was always the one listening to others and never the one others would listen to. I struggled with trusting myself.

My emotions were hidden, and my anxiety started to manifest itself more physically, as severe digestive issues. I saw so many gastroenterologists and received every medical test in the book. The diagnosis? Irritable bowel syndrome (IBS). What I learned was that IBS is basically a fancy term for "nothing is seriously wrong with your gut [thank goodness], but there is nothing more we can do." I felt alone, hopeless, and sick. With no one else to turn to but the internet, I started to research more about holistic healing and Eastern medicine. I began to find hope in what I was learning about the mind-body-spirit connection.

I felt a sense of belonging when I would show up for a weekly yoga class. I found comfort in guided meditations, breathwork, and self-soothing exercises. I practiced setting boundaries with others and challenged myself to talk openly about my feelings when I felt safe to do so. I found a therapist who believed in holistic psychology as much as I did and trusted in my recovery. I didn't know it at the time, but I was in the process of creating my own anxiety-healing tool kit. I am now more aware of the tools I need when anxiety shows up and I begin to feel out of control. I created this resource guide complete with every tool and technique that has contributed to my own healing journey in hopes of helping you create the tool kit that will lead you on your own road to recovery.

THE ANXIETY HEALER

Yes, I am a licensed therapist who specializes in anxiety. In fact, I was voted "most likely to be a therapist" in the eighth grade. Yep, you heard that right. I have been unintentionally helping people heal and recover since middle school. Back then, the title didn't really have much meaning, but today it is one of the only things in my life that makes sense. I have always had an innate drive to help others. I always knew I wanted to be some type of healer, but I wasn't sure if it was possible. I always doubted myself. I never felt that what I said actually mattered. That was until early 2018, when "The Anxiety Healer" social media profile was born. As I started to share more about my anxiety-healing journey on Instagram, people from around the world became invested in my recovery, as well as my expertise as a therapist. I started posting to raise more awareness about anxiety with holistic healing remedies; cognitive behavioral techniques; gut health practices; and, most important, educational self-help stories.

My hope was to create a healing community where others could find the support I wish I had as an anxious child, teenager, college student, and adult. What started as a small personal page with a positive saying or inspirational quote here and there became a place for anxiety sufferers from around the world to connect and feel less alone in their mental health struggles. In just three years, my healing page has become a source of education, community, advocacy, and a place to find mental health resources worldwide. I put my heart and soul into every single post, story, and reel that I create, just as I am doing with this healing guide. I bring my expertise as a licensed therapist and, more important, as a human on her own road to recovery. I am not a "superior being" just because I have credentials behind my name. I am human first, therapist second.

I know you feel lost. I know that you're scared. I feel your pain. I see your struggle. I write this book from a place of love and compassion. As someone who is highly sensitive, I feel so much of what others feel and I know how hard this healing journey is. You will have good days and bad days. You will have days when you will want to give up. You may feel discouraged if the first couple of exercises don't work. But remember, healing is not linear. It's all part of the journey, and I believe in you. This is the first step of the rest of your life. You are not alone. YOU GOT THIS!

WHO IS THIS GUIDE FOR?

I have created this guide for my fellow recoverers who courageously show up every day ready to face their fears. Healers who continuously fight for their right to feel at peace. Former sufferers who understand that there is no "quick fix" to healing anxiety and that it takes commitment to show up and do the work every day. Healers who are ready to take control of their life, stare anxiety in the face, and say, "I refuse to let you win today." This guide is for everyone who believes that healing is possible despite setbacks or naysayers.

The anxiety-healing Instagram community has played an integral part in creating this guide, inspiring me to write a book that is full of practical, hands-on, real-life tools that can be used to lessen anxiety in everyday life. Tools that I have been using to help heal my own anxiety and in my private practice for more than twenty years. My goal for this holistic healing guide is to help you find what coping exercises, strategies, and techniques work best for you in times of high anxiety so you can create your own healing tool kit, along with advocating for professional support if needed.

HOW TO USE THIS GUIDE

This book is designed as a step-by-step handbook to help you conquer your anxiety anytime, anywhere. To make it comprehensive and easy to use, it is broken into categories including body breakthroughs, mind tricks to ease anxiety, and creating your own healing tool kit. As you practice the exercises in this book, you will begin to learn more about what strategies are most effective for you and how to create the best healing tool kit for your needs. These tools are meant to be used daily as part of your wellness routine. Remember, just because you have practiced one technique regularly doesn't mean that you are "cured" of anxiety. There is no one strategy that will magically take away all of your anxiety, so if the first tool you use doesn't seem to help or needs a "boost," practice another one, and then another.

With each new chapter I provide "on the go" activities and bonus healing exercises that will help to keep you feeling more in control of your recovery. This will help you to apply these new practices into your everyday life. If you are dedicated to reducing your anxiety, practice these tools daily, even when your anxiety feels manageable. The more you practice these skills, the more you will notice an improvement in your mood overall. I promise.

Remember: mental health healing is best achieved with the help of a therapist you feel supported by, safe with, and connected to. If it becomes difficult to complete your responsibilities daily, please seek professional help.

STEP 1: EDUCATE YOURSELF
WHAT IS ANXIETY?

Anxiety is a normal human emotion characterized by fear, worry, or uncertainty. Most of us stress regularly about things such as money, work, school, relationships, and family, but afterward we usually calm down and feel better. When you struggle with generalized anxiety, the feelings of fear and worry never seem to subside. Your anxious thought patterns are continuous, and you constantly feel "on edge."

When we are faced with stressful situations, our brains sometimes go into overdrive and we can feel as though something isn't right. That burst of anxiety typically occurs when we react to thinking about a potentially threatening situation and our brain automatically creates a catastrophic response. Most times these thoughts are unrealistic, and while we can't predict the future, our brains trick us into believing that we can—and always goes right to the worst-case scenario.

When you suffer with anxiety, those brain signals create more fear and less rational thinking patterns. Our brains want those difficult thoughts and feelings to go away, so we are much more alert, and it feels nearly impossible to think about anything else. Our bodies then respond with things such as a racing heart, upset stomach, headache, muscle tightness, shortness of breath, or any number of other physical symptoms that may feel debilitating at that moment.

To help create a sense of calm and peace, you have to train your mind and body to become more mindful by focusing more and more on the present moment. This guide will teach you all of the tools, techniques, and strategies you need to create a less anxious mind and a more balanced way of living.

THE MIND-BODY CONNECTION
Panic Attack vs. Anxiety Attack

You've likely heard the phrases "panic attack" and "anxiety attack" used interchangeably. Both anxiety attacks and panic attacks have similar symptoms, causes, and risk factors. So what exactly is the difference between a panic attack and an anxiety attack? The bottom line is that symptoms can be very similar in nature, but panic attacks tend to be more intense and often have more severe physical symptoms. Panic attacks can come on fast, sometimes out of nowhere, and peak within ten minutes or so.[1] A panic attack may feel so strong and scary that some people may mistake it for a fatal heart attack. The truth is that you cannot die from a panic attack! Whether having a panic attack or an anxiety attack, this healing guide will provide you with the tools you need to remain grounded and calm.

Physical Symptoms of Anxiety

Does the following sound familiar? You feel dizzy and light-headed often. It is difficult to eat a full meal, not because you feel full but because your

---

1   "Panic Attacks," University of Pennsylvania, December 11, 2020, https://www.med.upenn.edu/ctsa/panic_symptoms.html.

stomach feels like it is at capacity and you can't take another bite. You notice that things don't even seem real, and it's as if you're floating above your body. Your heart starts to race. Your muscles tense. You're dizzy, and sweat is pouring down your back. You begin shaking. You try to take some deep breaths, look at your surroundings while relaxing each muscle in your body one at a time, but still you can't stop shaking. You feel like you swallowed a brick and try to take sips of water to keep yourself from throwing up, but it is hard to swallow. You are thinking, *Am I dying? What is wrong with me?*

What if I told you that there is a good chance that despite those very real physical symptoms, you are as healthy as can be? Would you believe me? Probably not, because something in your mind is telling you that you aren't . . . *and that "thing" is called anxiety!*

Most people are familiar with the idea that anxiety is a "mental" problem and view it as only a deep sense of debilitating fear, worry, and concern. While this is somewhat true, anxiety has many physical symptoms as well . . . some that can be identified even when fearsome or worried thoughts are not present.

For some of us, it is easier to recognize some of the classic signs of anxiety such as shortness of breath, racing heart, and constant overthinking. What's also important is to know of the debilitating physical impact anxiety has on the body.

Physical symptoms associated with anxiety include (but are not limited to):

- Increased heart rate
- Shortness of breath
- Sweating
- Shaking
- Nausea
- Hyperventilation
- Chest pain
- Light-headedness
- Fainting
- Muscle weakness

- Feeling of choking or throat tightening
- Muscle tension such as clenching your jaw
- Feeling weak or tired
- Sweating
- Hot flashes
- Chills
- Dry mouth
- Headache
- Gastrointestinal symptoms such as nausea, cramping, or diarrhea
- Increased frequency of need to urinate

WHY THE BRAIN CREATES PHYSICAL PAIN

Are you ready for a science lesson? Just kidding, but it's important to know why the body responds the way it does when we are anxious. When we are in danger, the eyes or ears (or both) send information to an area of the brain that contributes to emotional processing called the amygdala. The amygdala interprets images and sounds, and when it perceives danger, it instantly sends a distress signal to the hypothalamus. The hypothalamus is the area of the brain that communicates with the rest of the body through the autonomic nervous system (ANS), which basically regulates the body's response to anxiety. The ANS controls involuntary body functions such as breathing, blood pressure, and heartbeat. The ANS is made up of two components, the sympathetic nervous system and the parasympathetic nervous system.[2]

Sympathetic Nervous System (Fight or Flight)

The sympathetic nervous system functions like a gas pedal in a car and triggers the fight-or-flight response. With sympathetic nervous responses, the body speeds up, then tenses up, and then becomes more alert so it can respond to perceived dangers. The problem is, even in situations that are not dangerous, those who suffer from anxiety will still have the same response.

---

2 "Understanding the Stress Response," Harvard Medical School, July 6, 2020, https://www.health.harvard.edu/staying-healthy/understanding-the-stress-response.

This is because when you feel anxious, your brain floods your nervous system with adrenaline and cortisol, two chemicals that help you respond to a threat. In the short term, this increases your pulse and breathing rate so your brain can get more oxygen. An anxiety disorder can create a false sense of reality, which means that your brain most likely perceives certain nonthreatening situations as dangerous, causing the sympathetic nervous system to be activated.

Parasympathetic Nervous System (Rest and Digest)

The parasympathetic nervous system, on the other hand, acts like a brake. It promotes the "rest and digest" response that calms the body down after the danger has passed. To activate the parasympathetic nervous system, we have to practice doing so.

The best way to activate the parasympathetic nervous system is to practice strategies that stimulate the vagus nerve, known as the "communication highway" between the brain and the body, which represents the main component of the parasympathetic nervous system. The vagus nerve oversees a number of crucial bodily functions, including digestion, heart rate, breathing, control of mood, and immune response.[3] Its main function is to tell the body when it's time to relax and destress, but sometimes the vagus nerve needs to be stimulated to see long-term improvements in mood, well-being, and resilience. By increasing your "vagal tone," meaning the vagus nerve's activity, you can help reduce inflammation in the body and better regulate the stress response. This guide provides many different exercises that have been shown to increase vagal tone.

While everyone experiences anxiety from a different lens, many people often feel so out of control that they may be unable to stop shaking, have muscle aches, or get hot flashes, chills, tingly arms and legs, fatigue, indigestion, or headaches. These physical responses can feel quite frightening when they happen, but I promise they are not dangerous (this is assuming you have had the doctor rule out any other medical conditions). The truth is, the physical symptoms that occur when we are anxious are very real, but the thoughts behind them may not be. Step 2 will help you to become

---

3   Sigrid Breit et al., "Vagus Nerve as Modulator of the Brain-Gut Axis in Psychiatric and Inflammatory Disorders," *Frontiers in Psychiatry* 9 (March 2018): 44.

more aware of the patterns of your anxiety. Learning how to rate your anxiety daily will become an integral part of your healing.

STEP 2: RATE YOUR ANXIETY

To become more familiar with your triggers and patterns of anxiety, it is important to begin to rate your level of intensity every day. This will help you become more familiar with the events or situations that create anxiety and give you a reference point as to when exactly you should begin using your healing skills. Knowing more about your daily anxiety levels and how to identify the best time to use the tools provided in this guide will aid you in regulating your anxious mind and body.

This is all part of being self-aware. Self-awareness, or conscious awareness, is so important to our mental health healing because it can shine a light on the parts of our internal world (thoughts, feelings, physical sensations) that might otherwise get buried deep, pushed aside, or go unnoticed. Self-awareness is a form of stepping back and observing thoughts and feelings as they unfold, which is the first step toward change and growth. The more aware you become of what situations or environments trigger your anxiety, the more control you will have over how long it lasts!

USING THE RATING SCALE

Use the following rating scale daily. Write down in a journal what was happening to your body as you moved from a 2, 3, 4, 5, and so on. Also try to identify the thought patterns that may be influencing this fear or worry.

Example:

> Sarah woke up at 3:30 a.m. and couldn't get back to sleep. She had to be up for work at 7:00 a.m. Sarah knows that she feels irritable and anxious when she doesn't sleep well, and she also has a huge presentation at work that day. Sarah got out of bed at 6:30 a.m. and immediately rated her anxiety at a 4. Sarah knew that she would soon be a 5 or a 6 once she got into her car and started driving to work. Sarah decided to look into her healing tool kit and practice a couple of strategies. Sarah completed a ten-

Anxiety Rating Scale

RATE YOUR ANXIETY FROM 1–10

MILD

1 **Everything is A-OK!** You're the calmest you have ever been! You're probably smiling and feeling happy! (Pick any healing tool to practice today.)

2 **You are slightly worried or scared.** You're easily distracted and cheered up with little effort. (Use at least one tool from your healing tool kit today.)

3 **You're mildly worried.** Things are bothering you, but you're coping. You might be tired or have a headache. (Use 1-2 tools from your tool kit throughout the day.)

4 **Today is a bad day. You still have the skills to get through it.** You may need some extra self-care strategies. (Use 1-3 healing tools from your tool kit throughout the day.)

5 **You're moderately worried and starting to feel more physical pain.** Easy things are becoming difficult and it may be hard to use your healing tools. (Use 2-3 healing tools throughout the day.)

6 **Your worry is starting to take over.** Physical symptoms are present but manageable. You are unable to do things the way you usually do them. You may want to reach out for some support. (Use 2-3 healing tools throughout the day.)

7 **You are feeling more out of control.** You may experience more intense physical symptoms, including racing heart, shortness of breath, and stomach upset. This is more serious.

8 **You are unable to control yourself.** You begin to believe that you will not survive. Physical symptoms become worse.

9 **You aren't functioning anymore and need urgent help.** You need your support system. You body may be shaking and feeling disconnected from reality.

SEVERE

10 **The worst panic attack you've ever had. You end up in the ER.** You can no longer take care of yourself and can't imagine things getting any worse.

Anxiety Rating Scale (Healing Guide)

RATE YOUR ANXIETY FROM 1–10

MILD

1 Everything is A-OK! — Pick any healing tool to practice today.

2 You are slightly worried or scared. — Use at least 1 healing tool today.

3 You're mildly worried. — Practice 1-2 healing tools.

4 Today is a bad day. You still have the skills to get through it. — Practice 2-3 healing tools.

5 You're moderately worried and starting to feel more physical pain. — Practice 2-3 healing tools twice a day.

6 Your worry is starting to take over. — Practice at least 3 healing tools twice a day.

7 You are feeling more out of control. — Call for support.

8 You are unable to control yourself. — Call for support.

9 You aren't functioning anymore and need urgent help. — Seek professional help.

10 The worst panic attack you've ever had. You end up in the ER. — Seek professional help and possible psychiatrist referral.

SEVERE

minute guided meditation specifically tailored for work stress relief and also reminded herself to practice square breathing. After this, Sarah's anxiety went down to a 3 and she felt ready to take on the workday. Sarah also continued to practice deep breathing and took several breaks throughout the day to get some fresh air. Before the presentation Sarah practiced positive self-talk and said to herself in the bathroom mirror, "You got this, and if you make a mistake, don't worry. I still love you, and you are a rock star." Sarah's anxiety never went above a 4 the rest of the day.

STEP 3: EMOTIONAL AWARENESS

If we're lucky, as we grow up we become more aware of our feelings and *why* those feelings affect us in a certain way. This is known as emotional awareness or emotional intelligence. Being aware of emotions helps us to relate to other people, regulate our response to adversity, and make sound choices. Even emotions we may consider "negative" (e.g., fear, anger, or sadness) can give us insight into ourselves and others. Emotional awareness comes more easily to some people than others for a number of reasons, including (but not limited to) history of trauma, emotional immaturity of parents or caregivers, or lack of education around emotional regulation. The good news is that it is a skill that anyone can learn and practice.

Here are some ways to practice becoming more attuned to your inner emotions:

1. **Name your emotions.** Start by just noticing different emotions as you feel them, and then give the emotion a name. Try to use an "I" statement such as "I feel [feeling word]." For example, "I feel sad," "I feel disappointed," "I feel worried," and so on.
2. **Get to know your emotions.** Check out the list of feeling words provided and practice building your emotional vocabulary.

How Are You Feeling?

Happy   Embarrassed   Scared   Nervous   Goofy   Surprised

Quiet   Annoyed   Cool   Sad   Tired   Excited

Bored   Sick   Frustrated   Angry   Funny   Proud

3. **Keep a feelings journal.** Take a few minutes each day to write about how you feel and why. Journaling about your experiences and feelings builds emotional awareness.

4. **Notice how often you feel a specific emotion.** Try to make a mental note (or you can take note in your feelings journal) when a specific emotion shows up for you. Note and rate the intensity of the emotion. What is the level of your anger, from 1 (hardly angry at all) to 10 (the angriest I have ever felt)? Notice where you are, who you're with, and what you're doing when that emotion is present. This will also help to build emotional consciousness.

STEP 4: RECOGNIZE YOUR THOUGHT PATTERNS

This step is one of the most important steps when it comes to rewiring the anxious brain. You will learn all about irrational thought patterns and gain insight into how to recognize a "fear-based brain." The "fear-based brain" creates anxiety by distorting reality and persevering on irrational fears.

WHAT IS COGNITIVE BEHAVIORAL THERAPY (CBT)?

Cognitive behavioral psychologist Dr. Aaron Beck theorized that our emotions are created due to the way we think. Cognitive behavioral therapy (CBT) is a structured, action-oriented type of psychological treatment that helps individuals with anxiety disorders identify their core beliefs and how they contribute to irrational thought patterns.[4] According to multiple sources in the psychology field, cognitive behavioral therapy takes a more proactive approach toward actually changing disordered ways of thinking and challenging limiting core beliefs.[5] Treatment includes rewiring the way these thoughts automatically respond to a perceived fearful situation, thus changing our emotional response and behaviors. Incorporating mindfulness-based strategies into this practice

4   "Cognitive Model," Beck Institute: Cognitive Behavioral Therapy, accessed November 21, 2020, https:// beckinstitute.org/cognitive-model/.
5   J. A. Cully and A. L. Teten, "A Therapist's Guide to Brief Cognitive Behavioral Therapy" (Houston: Department of Veterans Affairs, South Central MIRECC, 2008), https://depts.washington.edu/dbpeds /therapists_guide_to_brief_cbtmanual.pdf.

Butterfly Observation

THINK OF YOUR THOUGHTS AS
BUTTERFLIES FLUTTERING AROUND YOU

Observe the butterflies and become completely aware of
them, but don't pick out one butterfly over another.

You don't notice good of bad butterflies,
happy or sad ones, or ugly or beautiful ones.

You are simply aware they are there and
acknowledge their presence.

also can help to activate the parasympathetic nervous system and stimu-
late the vagus nerve, helping the mind and body relax. Many people who
struggle with their mental health find that using CBT helps to manage
irrational fears, relieve chronic anxiety, and improve quality of life.

COGNITIVE DISTORTIONS

There are a number of irrational thought patterns that are called "cognitive
distortions." These thought patterns are present in any anxiety-provoking
situation.[6] Look at the following list and see which cognitive distortions
you identify with the most. It can be one, a few, or all of them. After the
description of each distortion is a quote or quotes reflecting the thought
pattern during that distortion.

After identifying which cognitive distortion(s) you struggle with the
most, write an example of a thought of yours that matches.

- **Catastrophizing:** Imagining and believing that the worst
  possible outcome will happen. "I will never get through this."
  "I did horrible in that interview and will never get another
  job."
- **Overgeneralizing:** Drawing a conclusion based on a *single*
  event or a couple of experiences. "I failed this interview, so I
  will fail every other interview." "No one asked me to dance,
  so no one ever will."
- **Personalization:** You attribute a disproportionate amount of
  the blame for negative feelings events to yourself . . . you fail
  to see that certain events are also caused by others. "My mom
  is always upset. She would be fine if I did more to help her."
- **Jumping to conclusions:** Interpreting the meaning of a
  situation with little or no evidence.
    - **Mind reading:** Believing that you know what other
      people are thinking with no sufficient evidence. "She
      wouldn't go on a date with me. She probably thinks I'm
      ugly."

---

6   D. Clark and A. Beck, *The Anxiety and Worry Workbook: The Cognitive Behavioral Solution* (New York:
Guilford Press, 2012).

What Is CBT?

What is Cognitive Behavioral Therapy (CBT)?

The key idea behind cognitive behavioral therapy is that:

WHAT YOU THINK **AND** DO

AFFECT THE WAY YOU FEEL

CBT is "present-focused." That means it works with thoughts and feelings in the here and now. A cognitive behavioral therapist will try to understand a situation by looking at separate parts:

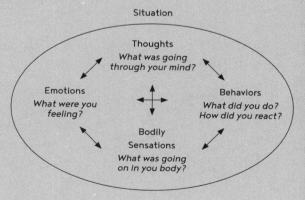

Situation

Thoughts
What was going through your mind?

Emotions
What were you feeling?

Behaviors
What did you do? How did you react?

Bodily Sensations
What was going on in you body?

What Is CBT?

Sometimes, through no fault of their own, people get "stuck" in vicious cycles: the things they do to solve a problem can inadvertently keep that problem going.

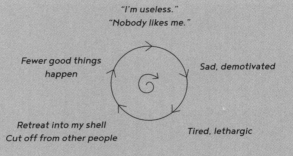

"I'm useless."
"Nobody likes me."

Sad, demotivated

Tired, lethargic

Retreat into my shell
Cut off from other people

Fewer good things
happen

CBT is about finding out what is keeping us "stuck" and making changes in our thinking and actions in order to improve the way we feel. It's a collaborative therapy and needs your active participation in order to be helpful. There is a lot of evidence showing that it's an effective treatment.

The Anxiety Healer's Guide

THOUGHT LOG

Date and Time

Anxiety Rating (1–10)

Situation
Who? What? When? Where?

Emotions
What emotions did you feel?

Automatic Thought(s)
What was going through your mind just before you started feeling anxious? (Circle the most intrusive thought.)

Cognitive Distortion
Which cognitive distortion best supports your irrational thought?

Evidence Against Thoughts
That DOES NOT support the triggered automatic thought(s).

Alternative Thought
Write an alternative or balanced thought.

New Anxiety Rating (1–10)

- **Fortune-telling:** Expecting a situation will turn out badly without adequate evidence. "The plane I'm about to get on will crash." "I'll fail this interview." "I'll get sick at this party."
- **Emotional reasoning:** The assumption that emotions reflect the way things really are and you let your feelings guide your interpretation of reality. "I feel guilty, therefore I must have done something bad." "I feel scared, therefore this must be dangerous."
- **Disqualifying the positive:** Recognizing only the negative aspects of a situation while ignoring the positive. One might receive many compliments on an evaluation but focus on the single piece of negative feedback. "Many people liked my presentation, but I stumbled giving the intro, so it was bad."
- **"Should" statements:** The belief that things should be a certain way. You focus on the way things "should" be instead of focusing on what is. "I should do well. If I don't, then I'm a failure." "I should go to the party or else my friends will be mad at me."
- **All-or-nothing thinking:** Thinking in absolutes such as "always," "never," or "every." "I never do a good enough job on anything." "I always ruin everything."
- **What if:** You keep asking a series of questions about "what if" something happens, and you fail to be satisfied with any of the answers. "What if I get anxious?" or "What if I can't catch my breath?"
  - ☐ Catastrophizing: _____
  _____

  - ☐ Overgeneralizing: _____
  _____

  - ☐ Personalization: _____
  _____

  - ☐ Jumping to conclusions: _____
  _____

- ☐ Mind reading: _____

  _____

- ☐ Fortune-telling:_____

  _____

- ☐ Emotional reasoning: _____

  _____

- ☐ Disqualifying the positive: _____

  _____

- ☐ "Should" statements: _____

  _____

- ☐ All-or-nothing thinking: _____

  _____

- ☐ What if: _____

  _____

CONNECTING EMOTION WITH THOUGHT

Complete this statement:

I feel _____ [feeling word] because I think _____.

COGNITIVE RESTRUCTURING
CBT Thought Log Exercise

Complete the thought log on page xxvii daily and become more comfortable with the distorted thought patterns.

STEP 5: IDENTIFY YOUR TRIGGERS
TYPES OF ANXIETY TRIGGERS

Recognizing the triggers that activate anxiety episodes is going to play a huge role in our healing. Once we are able to identify what people, events, or situations create an intense fear in our mind, we are then able to identify the source of our anxiety. A number of things that may trigger our anxiety, including:

- Large crowds
- Abuse

- Work
- Fear of failure
- Poor performance
- Mistakes
- Home life
- Thoughts of the future
- Small spaces
- Fear of dying
- Animals
- Accidents
- Trauma
- Sleep
- Trying new things
- Meeting new people
- Confrontation
- Finances
- Family issues
- Forgetfulness
- Fear of being alone
- Fear of not being accepted
- Roller coasters
- Heights
- Maintaining conversations
- Illness

Although this is a good list to start with, it is up to you to look deeper into the thoughts that may be related to these fears. This will help you to become familiar with your triggers and what types of intrusive thoughts may be connected to them.

STEP 6: CREATE YOUR HEALING TOOL KIT

Now that you know more about your own thought patterns, triggers, and emotions, let's discover what healing tools work best for *you*. It's time to create your anxiety-healing tool kit! Chapter 9 is dedicated to this step-by-step process and provides instructions on how to create a recovery plan specific to your healing journey. I even share my own anxiety-healing tool kit with you and provide an example of how to categorize each healing practice. I am not lying when I tell you that I have tried every single healing tool in this book. Your anxiety-healing tool kit should be a combination of approaches that elicit the relaxation response, behavioral activation skills, and a support system. These include deep abdominal breathing techniques, grounding strategies, visualization exercises, self-soothing items, books, apps, distraction ideas, movement exercises, therapeutic supports, and so much more.

STEP 7: THE ANXIETY-HEALING TREATMENT PLAN

1. **Check in with yourself.** Always rate yourself before and after an exercise. Rate the level of your anxiety between 1 (very calm state) and 10 (the worst panic attack ever). What is the level of your distress when you begin? How much did it decrease after the exercise? This can help give you more insight as to which technique may be working best for you.

2. **Practice these strategies at the first sign of anxiety.** Don't wait to begin these healing strategies when you are at an anxiety level of 6, 7, or 8 because it will be 100 percent harder for you to come down from it. Remember, if a technique doesn't work at first, try to stick with it for a bit before moving on to another.

3. **Use this healing guide even when you feel calm.** It can help to use this guide even when you aren't experiencing distress. If you get used to an exercise before you need to use it, it may take less effort when you want to use it to cope in the moment. It also can help to create healthy habits of mindfulness and relaxation.

4. **Use this guide in conjunction with therapy.** This guide is not meant to cure anxiety or treat specific anxiety disorders. It is meant to help you feel more in control of your mind and body when you feel powerless. To get the most out of your

healing, it is recommended that you use this guide alongside the support of a mental health counselor.

5. **Check in with your support system.** A support system is going to be an integral part of your healing process. Learning how to set boundaries with those who trigger your anxiety may be hard, but it is vital to the healing process. Check in with those you feel the safest with consistently. As you become more emotionally attuned, practice speaking openly and honestly to these individuals about your feelings.

It took a lot of trial and error to establish what healing tools worked best for me, and I continue to learn as life happens. There is no "one size fits all" when it comes to healing anxiety, so it may be best to start practicing every technique in this guide and then narrow them down after you see what works best for you!

Along with rating your anxiety before and after each exercise, evaluate the tools that you practice by keeping track of which ones consistently decrease your level of anxiety. Remember, what works best for you may not work best for the next anxious person . . . so be patient with yourself and give yourself a huge hug for even beginning this healing journey! YOU GOT THIS and I AM SO PROUD OF YOU! Happy healing!

Part I

BODY

BREAKTHROUGHS

CHAPTER 1

The Breathing Solution

I f you're reading this, chances are you have experienced a panic attack at some point in your life. Or, if you have not experienced a panic attack, then you have probably experienced an anxiety attack. The difference between the two is not widely known, but there is one. Panic attacks often come on suddenly and involve an intense and often overwhelming fear. They are accompanied by a number of physical symptoms, including racing heartbeat, dizziness, shortness of breath, and nausea. On the other hand, an anxiety attack is usually related to the anticipation of a stressful situation, experience, or event and may be less intense and come on gradually.

Because anxiety attacks are not recognized as a diagnosis in the *DSM-5* (the *DSM* is basically the essential guide for how psychotherapists diagnose their clients), the signs and symptoms of those who experience one may look very different. Two people may suffer an "anxiety attack" but have completely different physical, behavioral, or emotional symptoms. One thing that is for sure: whether you are having a panic attack or an anxiety attack, the body always responds physically. Some of these physical symptoms include an upset stomach, racing heart, dizziness, heart palpitations, muscle tension, throat tightness, light-headedness, and the one that never fails to scare us the most: shortness of breath! So in these moments it is important to remember that the mind and the body are connected! As much as you may think it at the time, the physical symptoms we experience when we are in a state of high anxiety are not dangerous at all, and you will never die from a panic attack.

THE SCIENCE OF BREATHING

There are two parts of the autonomic nervous system: the sympathetic nervous system (fight or flight) and the parasympathetic nervous system (rest and digest). When you have a panic attack or an anxiety attack, the sympathetic nervous system is activated and you experience a whole range of physical symptoms, including rapid heart rate, heart palpitations, and shortness of breath.[1] This response sometimes occurs so fast that people often don't realize it's happening! As discussed in the introduction, stimulating the vagus nerve can help activate the parasympathetic nervous system. To stimulate the vagus nerve, it's important to practice lengthening and deepening our breathing patterns. This is why creating a daily habit of breathwork is so important in healing anxiety.

When you're faced with a dangerous situation, your brain floods your nervous system with chemicals such as adrenaline and cortisol, which are designed to help you respond to a threat. When these chemicals are released, your pulse and breathing rate increase. The only problem is, when you're in a state of high anxiety, there is most likely no threatening situation. You are perceiving it as such . . . thus creating this intense fear and activating the sympathetic nervous system (fight or flight). To come back down to a calm and balanced state, you need to practice strategies that activate the parasympathetic nervous system (rest and digest)—especially deep, slow breathing. When you practice deep breathing the oxygen breathed in stimulates the body's parasympathetic nervous system.

This, in turn, produces a feeling of calmness and body connectedness that diverts attention from stressful, anxious thoughts and quiets what's going on in the mind. When the parasympathetic nervous system is activated your metabolism decreases, your heart beats slower, your muscles

---

[1] Lurie Kelly McCorry, "Physiology of the Autonomic Nervous System," *American Journal of Pharmaceutical Education* 71, no. 4 (August 2007): 78, doi:10.5688/aj710478.

Rectangle Breathing

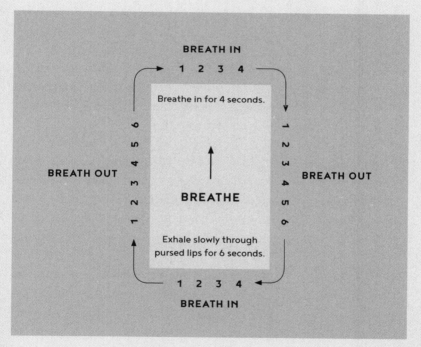

relax, your breathing becomes slower, and even your blood pressure decreases.

The breathing techniques in this chapter have been shown to help calm the nervous system, counteract stress, and reduce negative emotions.[2] It is suggested to practice at least one to two of these breathing techniques daily (even when not feeling anxious) to get into the habit of breathing from your diaphragm more slowly and deeply.

HEALING IN ACTION
RECTANGLE BREATHING
How to Practice Rectangle Breathing

Recommended practice: any time you begin to feel anxious. Rectangle breathing is a technique used to help slow down your heart rate. This method helps to divert your attention from the irrational thought patterns that create anxiety. While this may not be a long-term solution to healing anxious thoughts, this breathing technique can at least help with shortness of breath.

1. Breathe in through your nose for a count of 4.
2. Breathe out through your mouth for a count of 6.
3. Breathe in through your nose for a count of 4.
4. Breathe out through your mouth for a count of 6.

LION'S BREATH
How to Practice Lion's Breath

Recommended practice: practice lion's breath two to three times a day to help alleviate stress, eliminate toxins, and stimulate your throat and upper chest. Lion's breath involves exhaling forcefully through your mouth, as if you were roaring like a lion.

- Sit in a comfortable position with your hands on your knees and your ankles crossed.

---

2   Ravinder Jerath et al., "Self-Regulation of Breathing as a Primary Treatment for Anxiety," *Applied Psychophysiology and Biofeedback* 40, no. 2 (June 2015): 107–15, doi: 10.1007/s10484-015-9279-8.

- Stretch out your arms and your fingers.
- Take a deep breath in through your nose.
- During exhale . . . open your mouth as wide as you can and stick your tongue out, stretching it down toward your chin as far as it will go and release the breath while making a *HA* sound.
- Focus on the middle of your forehead or the end of your nose while exhaling.
- Relax your face as you inhale again.
- Repeat the practice up to six times, changing the cross of your ankles when you reach the halfway point.

Google keywords: lion's breath for anxiety

Bonus Healing Activity

Practice lion's breath at least three times per day. Schedule specific times when you will practice lion's breath daily and set a timer in your smartphone.

DIAPHRAGMATIC (BELLY) BREATHING

Diaphragmatic breathing or "belly" breathing is one of my favorite breathing tools. This specific type of breathwork can help to activate your relaxation response and allows the respiratory system to function correctly. When anxiety arises, our breathing can become shallow and erratic. Practicing belly breathing allows the mind and body to slow down and relax. When we breathe deeply through our abdominals, the oxygen taken in stimulates the body's parasympathetic nervous system and activates the rest and digest part of our brain. This then creates a feeling of calm within our body and mind, which diverts attention from stressful, anxious thoughts. According to the American Institute of Stress, practicing diaphragmatic breathing or "belly" breathing for twenty to thirty minutes a day can help reduce anxiety.[3]

---

3   Kellie Marksberry, "Take a Deep Breath," American Institute of Stress, August 10, 2012, https://www
.stress.org/take-a-deep-breath.

How to Practice Diaphragmatic (Belly) Breathing

Recommended practice: twenty to thirty minutes per day.

Here's the basic procedure for diaphragmatic breathing:

1. Sit in a comfortable position or lie flat on the floor, your bed, or another comfortable, flat surface.
2. Place one hand on your chest and the other on your stomach. This will allow you to feel your belly move as you breathe. Relax your shoulders.
3. Breathe in slowly through your nose for about three seconds so that your stomach moves out against your hand (the hand on your chest should remain as still as possible).
4. You should feel the air move through your nostrils and down into your stomach, making your stomach expand. During this type of breathing, make sure your stomach is moving outward while your chest remains relatively still.
5. Open your mouth, press gently on your stomach, and exhale slowly for three seconds.

Complete at least three rounds.

Belly Beathing Benefits

- Helps you relax by lowering the harmful effects of the stress hormone cortisol on your body.
- Lowers your heart rate and blood pressure.
- Helps you cope with the symptoms of anxiety.
- Improves your core muscle stability.
- Improves your body's ability to tolerate intense exercise.
- Lowers your chances of injuring or wearing out your muscles.
- Slows your rate of breathing so it expends less energy.

Put a reminder notification in your smartphone to practice belly breathing at least three to four times per day. Gradually increase the amount of time you spend doing this exercise, and perhaps even increase the effort of the exercise by placing a book on your stomach.

ZEN WORD BREATHING

This exercise will identify superficial breathing and train your body to breathe deeply by using your diaphragm.

How to Practice Zen Word Breathing

Recommended practice: one to two times per day. Begin this exercise by thinking of a word that brings you peace and joy. Place one hand on your stomach and the other hand over your heart. Take a deep breath in through your nose and out through your mouth.

- Focus on the breath as the belly rises and falls.
- As you take in another breath, repeat your word in your mind.
- As you exhale, repeat your word again in your mind.
- As you take in another breath, slowly spell your word in your mind.
- Exhale and watch your belly fall as you spell your word in your mind.
- Continue to breathe in and out for ten counts total.

Bonus Healing Activity

Words that bring me peace and joy are _____.

STAR BREATHING EXERCISE

Use the star on the next page to slow your breathing.

Star Breathing

Follow the shape of the star with your finger and slowly follow the breathing pattern.

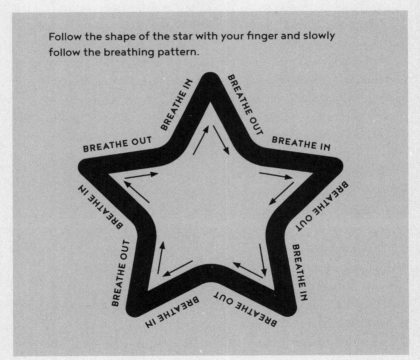

THE BELLOWS BREATHING TECHNIQUE:
AN ENERGY BOOSTER

Bellows breathing, or *bhastrika*, is adapted from a yogic breathing technique that aims to raise vital energy and increase alertness. This practice consists of a series of active inhalations and exhalations. According to Yoga International,

> Bellows breathing uses the action of the abdominal muscles and diaphragm to draw air in and out of the lungs, generating heat in the body by squeezing blood through the digestive organs, toning the liver, spleen, stomach, and pancreas, and increasing digestive capacity.[4]

If bellows breathing is done properly, you may feel as energized much in the same way that you feel after a good workout! You should feel the effort at the back of the neck, the diaphragm, the chest, and the abdomen. So instead of reaching for that next cup of coffee, try this breathing exercise the next time you need an energy boost!

How to Practice Bellows Breathing

Recommended practice: two to three times per day, always on an empty stomach.

Disclaimer: Do not practice bhastrika breathing if you're pregnant, have an ulcer, hiatal hernia, chronic constipation, heart disease, high blood pressure, uncontrolled hypertension, epilepsy, seizures, or panic disorder. Avoid practicing bellows breath on a full stomach; wait at least two hours after eating.

Sit up tall and relax your shoulders. Take a few deep breaths into and out from your nose and expand your belly fully as you breathe. While keeping your mouth closed but relaxed, inhale and exhale rapidly and forcefully *through your nose only* at the rate of one second per cycle. This is a noisy breathing exercise, but that is part of what makes it so healing! Your breaths in and out should be equal in duration but as short as pos-

---

4   "Learn Bhastrika Pranayama (Bellows Breath)," Yoga International, https://yogainternational.com/article/view/learn-bhastrika-pranayama-bellows-breath.

sible. Make sure the breath is coming from your diaphragm and keep your head, neck, shoulders, and chest as still as you can while your belly moves in and out.

1. Round 1: For your first cycle, move through a round of ten bhastrika breaths.
2. Breath break: pause and breathe normally for fifteen to thirty seconds.
3. Round 2: Begin the next round with twenty bhastrika breaths.
4. Breath break: pause and breathe normally for another thirty seconds.
5. Round 3: Complete this last round with thirty bhastrika breaths.
6. Breath break: take a break and breathe naturally for three rounds, observing the sensations in your mind and body.

Note: Make sure to listen to your body during the practice. If you feel light-headed in any way, pause for a few minutes while breathing naturally. When the discomfort passes, try another round of bellows breathing, slower and with less intensity.

Google keywords: bellow breathing for anxiety, bellow breathing practice

Bonus Healing Activity

Use bellows breaths:

- Before a workout
- In the morning
- Before a run
- Before a yoga class

4-7-8 BREATHING TECHNIQUE: A GREAT
TECHNIQUE TO HELP YOU FALL ASLEEP

The 4-7-8 breathing technique is a breathing pattern developed by Dr. Andrew Weil, who describes this yogic technique as "a natural tranquilizer for the nervous system."[5] The 4-7-8 sequence of deep, rhythmic breathing is very relaxing and may actually help people to fall asleep. This breathing technique may seem like a subtle exercise when you first try it, but with repetition and practice it can help you to gain better control over your breathing. The best thing about this exercise is that it doesn't require any equipment, takes little time to do, and can be done anywhere!

How to Practice 4-7-8 Breathing

Recommended practice: at least two times per day, once as you are falling asleep.

Disclaimer: do not practice while driving.

If you feel a little light-headed when you first breathe this way, do not worry . . . it will pass! Do not do more than four breaths at one time for the first month of practice. Although you can do the exercise in any position, as you are learning, it is best to sit with your back straight.

1. Begin by placing the tip of your tongue just behind your upper front teeth, and keep it there through the entire exercise.
2. Close your mouth and inhale quietly through your nose to a mental count of 4.
3. Hold your breath for a count of 7.
4. Exhale completely through your mouth, making a whoosh sound to a count of 8.

Now inhale again and repeat the cycle three more times, for a total of four breaths.

Note: Some people may find it hard to breathe in for seven seconds and may become light-headed. You can do this exercise with a smaller

5 Andrew Weil, "Three Breathing Exercises and Techniques," May 2016, https://www.drweil.com /health-wellness/body-mind-spirit/stress-anxiety/breathing-three-exercises/.

Alternate Nostril Breathing

1

Close right nostril with thumb. Breathe in left nostril – 4 count

6

Open left nostril. Breathe out – 6 count

Calm your mind in 2 min.

ALTERNATE NOSTRIL BREATHING

repeat 6–8 x

2

Close both nostrils – 3 count

5

Close left nostril with ring finger. Breathe in right nostril – 4 count

3

Open right nostril. Breathe out – 6 count

4

Close both nostrils – 3 count

number of counts within the same ratio. For example, you can always use a 3-5-6 breathing pattern, and it will give you about the same effect.

ALTERNATE NOSTRIL BREATHING

Alternate nostril breathing is another technique used to activate the parasympathetic nervous system (calming the mind and body) and reduce blood pressure. Alternate nostril breathing may enhance respiratory strength, restore balance in the left and right hemispheres of the brain, rejuvenate the nervous system, and remove toxins.[6]

How to Practice Alternate Nostril Breathing

Recommended practice: daytime when you need to focus or relax (especially before or after a yoga class). Alternate nostril breathing is best done on an empty stomach. Don't practice alternate nostril breathing if you're sick or congested.

1. Place thumb gently on your right nostril (keep your left nostril open).
2. Inhale slowly and deeply through your left nostril.
3. Use your ring finger to close your left nostril (open your right nostril) and exhale through your right nostril.
4. Inhale through your right nostril.
5. Close your right nostril (open your left nostril) and exhale through your left nostril.

Take two normal breaths and start over again for up to five minutes.

USING YOUR IMAGINATION TO PRACTICE BREATHING

The point of this breathing exercise is to use your imagination and visualize these two objects when you become anxious. Close your eyes and picture your favorite flower. What does it look like? What color is it? What is the shape? How does it smell? Focus on the flower and take a long, slow breath in through your nose, smelling the flower. As you exhale, picture

---

6   Melissa Eisler, "Nadi Shodhana: How to Practice Alternate Nostril Breathing," Chopra, last modified November 15, 2015, https://chopra.com/articles/nadi-shodhana-how-to-practice-alternate-nostril-breathing.

yourself blowing the petals off the flower as if you are trying to slowly create a shower of flower petals.

Bonus Healing Activity

Find a real flower and describe the shape, smell, and texture:

_____

_____

_____

Draw your favorite flower:

BLOWING OUT THE CANDLES

Visualize a birthday cake with five lit candles. As you get ready to blow out the candles, take a deep breath in through your nose to a count of 5. When you're ready, blow out the candles as you pucker your lips and slowly exhale, counting to 5.

Write about your favorite birthday:

_____

_____

_____

Breathing Apps

- Apple Watch Breathe
- Breath Ball
- Breathe+Simple Breath Trainer

- Breathe2relax
- Breathe to Relax Pranayama App
- Breathly
- Breathwrk
- Breethe
- Calm
- DARE
- FearTools
- Headspace
- HitomiNow
- iBreathe
- Insight Timer
- Kardia
- Liberate
- Mindshift CBT
- MyStrength
- Power of Calm
- Rootd
- Sanvello
- Simple Habit
- Simply Being
- Smiling Mind
- Steady
- Stop, Breathe & Think
- Wim Hof Method

Still Trying to Catch Your Breath?

1. Put your hands together like you're praying, cup them over your mouth/nose, and create a small opening on the other side with your hands. The smaller airflow is much like breathing into a paper bag.

2. Create a small opening to breathe through by pressing the sides of your lips together.
3. Try to breathe with your stomach/diaphragm. Lying down flat on your back can help. Move to a firm surface if you're still having trouble.

KEYWORD PHRASES TO SEARCH ONLINE

Type these key phrases into Google or any other search engine and you will find thousands of videos, articles, and exercises that can be helpful when you are feeling anxious . . . no matter where you are!

- Breathing techniques for anxiety
- Calm the nervous system with breathing
- Breathwork for anxiety
- Activate the parasympathetic nervous system
- Breathing techniques for stress and anxiety
- How does breathing help anxiety?
- Why should I breathe slowly when I'm anxious?
- Simple breathing exercises to help calm down
- How to reduce anxiety with the breath
- How to relieve shortness of breath when anxious

BONUS HEALING EXERCISES

This is best completed using a journal to record daily and weekly breathwork. Practice as often as you can to create a more sustainable amount of healing. Consistent breathwork will not only help to decrease stress and anxiety over time but will also create a more balanced lifestyle.

My top three most healing breathing exercises are:

1. _____
2. _____
3. _____

Complete every morning.

I will practice _____ breathing technique at least _____ times today.

Set an alarm in your phone for at least three breath breaks throughout the day.

Breathwork time #1: _____

Breathwork time #2: _____

Breathwork time #3: _____

Weekly Breathwork Schedule

Complete at the beginning of every week.

I will practice _____ breathing technique at least _____ times this week.

Days I promise to practice breathwork this week (start with one to two days per week and gradually work your way up to seven days a week):

_____

Optional Journal Reflection

"I just completed my breathwork and I feel
_____."

"I just completed my breathwork and my body feels
_____."

Breathing Techniques to Add to My Tool Kit:

_____

_____

_____

CHAPTER 2

Peace at the Present Moment

This chapter is all about how to remain present in the moment while struggling with intrusive and ruminating anxious thoughts. Whether on the go or feeling anxious at home, school, or work, it's important that we expand our tool box of skills that helps us remain more mindful when life feels overwhelming or too difficult to handle. The practices in this chapter are called grounding techniques and will ultimately help create stillness in your overly active mind.

WHAT IS GROUNDING?

Grounding brings us into a state of reality (or mindfulness). Grounding techniques can help bring us back into the "here and now" in a safe way. The more present you are in your body, the calmer and safer you will feel. When you pay attention to what happens in your body, you become the captain of your mind. Grounding helps you become aware of what techniques are most healing for your nervous system. When grounding yourself, you are guiding your attention away from unsettling thoughts about the past and toward present safety.

You are probably familiar with the word "mindfulness," but what does it *really* mean? How does being more "mindful" lead to feeling less anxious? According to the founder of the Center for Mindfulness, Jon Kabat-Zinn, "mindfulness is a mental state achieved by focusing one's awareness on the present moment by paying attention, on purpose and without judgment. It is the act of acknowledging and accepting one's feelings, thoughts, and bodily sensations right here, right now."[1]

Mindfulness is vital when it comes to healing anxiety, because in a heightened state of anxiety, you may experience something called derealization or depersonalization.

- **Derealization** creates a feeling of detachment from your environment and the people in it. Your view of the world may seem distorted, and it may be difficult to focus on where you are at that moment. Practicing grounding during these episodes will bring you back to reality and help create a sense of safety.
- **Depersonalization** means you may feel as if you are an outside observer of your own thoughts or body. You may feel as though you are not in control of your thoughts or actions at the moment.

HOW TO USE THIS GROUNDING CHAPTER TO HELP HEAL ANXIETY

The techniques mentioned in this chapter can be useful when you are feeling highly anxious but should be practiced even when you are feeling calm. It is important to create a daily healing practice complete with cognitive tools, grounding exercises, and breathing techniques so that they will come naturally when you are upset or anxious. Grounding will help you to focus on some aspect of the present physical world rather than on your internal thoughts and feelings.

---

1 "What Is Mindfulness?" *Greater Good Magazine*, February 10, 2021, https://greatergood.berkeley.edu/topic/mindfulness/definition.

THE FIVE SENSES

The five senses grounding technique is highly recommended for anxiety because it can help bring your body out of a fight-or-flight state and back into the present moment. When you experience anxiety, your sympathetic nervous system goes into overdrive, which can cause intense feelings of panic, fear, or worry. When you're in panic mode, you lose the ability to think clearly—so bringing your mind to the sights, sounds, and smells around you can bring you back to reality and create a calmer state, both mentally and physically. Plus, this technique can be used anywhere!

Search for:

- Five things you can see
- Four things you can touch
- Three things you can hear
- Two things you can smell
- One thing you can taste

On-the-Go Activity

Make sure to have a notebook and pen or pencil with you (if not, you can use the notepad in your smartphone). Answer the following questions.

What are five things you can see?

- Pay attention to what you see around you and describe the items.
- What are their colors? Shapes? Patterns?

What are four things you can touch or feel?

- Notice the things around you that you can touch or feel.
- Do you feel the sun on your skin? What does the seat you are sitting on feel like?
- Maybe you have a self-soothing item with you. What does

it feel like? Describe its weight, texture, and other physical qualities.

- Can you describe four things on your body? Is there a sensation of clothing on your body, like your back against the chair, feet on the floor, or hair touching your neck?

What are three things you can hear?

- Pay special attention to the sounds around you and describe them.
- What do you hear? A ticking clock? An air conditioner? Cars in the distance? Wind? Music? People talking?

What are two things you can smell?

- Try to notice smells in the air around you and describe them.
- Air freshener? Grass? Is there anything around you that has a scent? flower? Candle? Essential oil?

What is one thing you can taste?

- Notice the taste or tastes in your mouth.
- What can you taste right now?
- It may help to carry something you can suck on or a small snack and focus your attention closely on the flavor or flavors.

THE SEVEN KEY QUESTIONS

Answer these questions to create a phrase that will help bring you back to the present moment. This will help direct your brain into a more mindful state of being when anxiety takes over.

- What is your name?
- How old are you?
- Where do you live?
- What are you wearing?
- What is today's date?
- Where are you at this moment?
- What do you notice around you?

Example:

I am Sally and I am twenty-four years old. I live in Philadelphia. I am wearing black sweatpants and a white long-sleeved top. I have a blue hat on, white socks, and tan sneakers. Today is June 3 and I am in the car with my sister. I can hear the moving cars around me, and the radio is on. I am safe at this moment and the time is 4:17 p.m.

On-the-Go Activity

Take out your smartphone or use a notepad to answer the questions above as though you are writing a story. After you answer the questions, continue writing the mantra "I am safe at this moment."

THE COUNTING DISTRACTION TECHNIQUE

Counting is another good way to help you relax. This technique involves writing numbers down on a dry eraseboard and then erasing them in your mind. You can also imagine a black curtain and watch the numbers appear and disappear. The act of having to keep track of numbers will help distract you.

1. Start by closing your eyes and picturing a huge whiteboard. The whiteboard can be as big as you are.
2. Now in your imagination, take a marker and write down the number 100 on the board as large as you can write it.

3. Then erase the number away as slowly as you can, making sure that the entire number is erased.
4. Write the number 99 next, then erase it very slowly.
5. Continue counting down until you feel calmer or reach 0 (or begin again).

GROUND YOURSELF WITH CATEGORIES

Try to choose at least two to three categories in the following list and name as many items as you can in each one.

- Movies
- Football teams
- Baseball teams
- Animals
- Colors
- Cities
- TV shows
- Cereals
- Fruits and vegetables
- Famous people

Bonus Healing Activity

Bring a notepad with you wherever you go and use it to write down your responses.

THE ANXIETY-HEALING GROUNDING SCRIPT

Anxiety may leave you feeling powerless, so use this affirming meditation to practice coaching yourself toward healing. Record this meditation in your own voice or have someone you feel safe with record it for you. Take this with you and listen to it (or watch if a video) any time you begin to feel anxious. Hearing your own voice will help you to internally talk to yourself in a more loving and encouraging way:

Close your eyes and take a deep breath in and a deep breath out.

Breathe in through your nose . . . 2 . . . 3 . . . 4

(pause)

And breathe out through your mouth . . . 2 . . . 3 . . . 4 . . . 5

(pause)

Remember that you are safe at this moment.

(pause)

You are safe at this moment.

(pause)

You are safe at this moment.

(pause)

No matter where your thoughts take you.

No matter what scary thoughts may come to your mind.

Remember, you are safe.

(pause)

Take a deep breath in for a count of 4.

(pause)

Hold it for 2.

(pause)

And breathe out for 6.

(pause)

When a scary thought pops into your head, remember that it is just a thought.

The thought has no power.

Watch the thought as if it were a cloud floating by.

(pause)

Observe the thought.

(pause)

Wave to the thought.

(pause)

And watch it float away.

(pause)

And remember . . . you are safe.

(pause)

Breathe in through your nose . . . 2 . . . 3 . . . 4 . . . hold . . .
2 . . . 3 . . . exhale through your mouth . . . 2 . . . 3 . . . 4 . . .
5 . . .

Breathe in through your nose . . . 2 . . . 3 . . . 4 . . . hold . . .
2 . . . 3 . . . exhale through your mouth . . . 2 . . . 3 . . . 4 . . .
5 . . .

Now as you relax . . . you can count your breaths as they continue to flow gently. Count 10 breaths.

(pause)

Notice the breath as it enters your nose.

Feel the breath as it passes through your nasal passages and down your throat.

Now, as you exhale through your mouth, notice as the air leaves your lungs.

(pause)

Observe how the breath flows slowly.

(pause)

You are safe.

You are safe at this moment.

Notice the calm state of your mind.

Notice that your body is relaxed and at peace.

On-the-Go Activity

Keep this recording saved on your phone and listen to it any time you begin to feel anxious. Bring headphones when you are traveling.

GROUND YOURSELF WITH A SELF-SOOTHING OBJECT

Many times, when you think of natural anxiety-relief tools, you may think of an online mental health program or a self-help book. While I am a huge advocate for both of those healing items, there are also a variety of comfort objects for anxiety that often go under the radar. It may be helpful to carry a grounding object in your pocket that you can touch whenever you feel triggered. I've done hours of research trying to compile a list of the best healing items that help reduce anxiety and create comfort in your surroundings. (You can find the complete list in chapter 4.) Here are some soothing items that can help get you through the day as you build good habits to manage your anxiety. These items may be helpful because they're soothing, calming, and enjoyable to fidget with.

Reminder: if you're suffering from (or think you may have) an anxiety disorder, please consult with a licensed counselor or doctor. These items can help you relieve some stress on a day-to-day basis but should not be used as replacements for prescribed anxiety treatments.

- Rock or leaf
- Crystal
- Essential oil
- Feather
- Squishy
- Stress ball
- Lyrics to a song or poem that brings you comfort (Healing tip: Write down the lyrics and take them with you)
- Essential oil accessory
- Mini Rubik's Cube
- Putty

On-the-Go Activity

Describe in detail the object you are holding. What is the object? What does it look like? How does it feel? What is the texture? What are the colors? What is the shape?

Repeat the mantra "I am safe here with this _____ [insert name of object]."

GROUNDING TECHNIQUES ANY TIME, ANYWHERE

It can be difficult to know how to control your anxiety when you are in environments that make you nervous. The truth is, there are ways to ground yourself no matter where you are. Having these grounding tools "in your back pocket" will leave you feeling more prepared and in control. One of the best tools that can be used anywhere is a coping card. You can either use an index card or the notepad on your smartphone to write down a couple of coping statements that you feel are *true* and that will help to remind you that your anxiety does not control you. Chapter 5 provides a huge list of effective coping statements to help reset the anxious brain. Another helpful grounding tool is one that you can touch. Choose a self-soothing item from the objects mentioned on the previous page (or from the list in chapter 4) and bring it with you wherever you go. Following are some examples of other grounding tools that may be helpful in different anxiety-provoking environments.

If you are at a party . . .

- Run your hands under cold water.
- Hold a piece of ice.
- Find a focus object and describe its shape, color, and what it does.
- Choose one or two broad categories and mentally list as many things as possible from each category: ice cream flavors, musical instruments, animals, TV shows, football teams, etc.
- Count the people in the room.
- Count backward from 100.

If you are in a car . . .

- Count the number of cars you pass.
- Count the number of trees out the window.
- Focus on the car in front of you.
- Hum a tune. (This will also stimulate the vagus nerve.)
- Count the number of yellow cars, blue cars, red cars, etc.
- Snap your fingers.
- Take a deep belly breath in through your nose and count for 4, hold your breath for 2, and take a slow breath out of your mouth for 6.

If you are on a bus or train . . .

- Count how many people you see with blond hair, brown hair, eyeglasses, hats, etc.
- Hum a tune. (This will also stimulate the vagus nerve.)
- Take 3 deep breaths in through your nose for a count of 4 and out through your mouth for a count of 4.
- List 10 things you are grateful for.
- Look around you and describe how many colors you see.
- Think, *I'm okay right now; at this moment, I am okay.*

If you are with your family . . .

- Count how many times someone uses the word "the" or "and."
- Bring a grounding object to keep in your pocket.
- Name every object that is yellow, blue, red, green, etc.
- Ask for a glass of cold water.
- Go to the bathroom and run your hands under cold water for 2 minutes.

If you are in a restaurant . . .

- Think, *I'm okay right now; at this moment, I am okay.*
- Take a deep breath, pause, and exhale.
- Shift your focus to the present moment by focusing on who you are with.
- Give yourself permission to take a break and go outside. Take 3 deep breaths.
- Go to the bathroom and run your hands under cold water for 2 minutes.
- Talk back to your anxiety and say, "You don't control me."

If you are at the doctor's office . . .

- Describe the waiting room. What do you see? What do you hear?

- Play a distraction game (review chapter 7).
- Bring a support person with you.
- Breathe in for 4. Hold for 2. Breathe out for 6.
- Count the pictures on the wall. What do the pictures look like?
- Use the bathroom and splash cold water on your face.

EVERYDAY GROUNDING

Use this list if you are trying to find a way to ground yourself right now. These techniques can be used to find more healing at this very moment.

- List five things you're thankful for.
- Count to 10 or say the alphabet. Very slowly.
- Notice your body. What are you wearing? How does your shirt feel on your chest? Wiggle your toes and feel the chair against your back.
- Dig your heels into the floor, literally "grounding" them! Notice the tension centered in your heels as you do this. Remind yourself that you are connected to the ground.
- Describe the steps in performing an everyday activity. For example, how to make your bed, do the dishes, cook your favorite meal, prepare your favorite meal, or tie a knot.
- Think of the names of your friends or family members. How many can you name? How old are they? Can you spell their names?
- Read something around you. Read the letters aloud forward and backward.
- Think of an object and "draw" it in your mind, or in the air with your finger. Try drawing fruit, a car, a house, or an animal.

Type these key phrases into Google or any other search engine and you will find thousands of grounding videos, articles, and exercises that can be helpful when you are feeling anxious—no matter where you are!

- Five senses grounding technique for anxiety
- Anxiety grounding tool to use in the car (do not use while driving)
- Body scan for anxiety
- Grounding techniques for PTSD
- Grounding techniques for social anxiety
- Progressive muscle relaxation for anxiety
- Reality testing for anxiety
- Affirmations for panic
- Grounding techniques for panic disorder
- Grounding techniques for OCD
- How to ground myself when I feel anxious
- Best grounding tools to use for anxiety

GROUNDING TOOLS TO PUT INTO
MY ANXIETY-HEALING TOOL KIT

_____

_____

_____

_____

_____

_____

_____

_____

_____

_____

_____

CHAPTER 3

Two Minutes to Be Panic-Free

When you begin to feel that the symptoms of anxiety or a panic attack are coming on, it can feel like you're losing control very easily, right? When we panic, our nervous system goes into overdrive, so it's important to recognize what we can do to calm the nervous system and restore balance in our mind and body. To help you on that journey, this chapter includes techniques that can help calm the nervous system in less than two minutes. Using these techniques does not guarantee that anxiety will be gone for good, but when practiced regularly these tools can help create a less anxious mind and a more restful body.

REMINDER!

Remember to rate your anxiety daily. When you wake up, look at the rating scale in the beginning of this book and ask yourself *What number am I this morning?* Doing this every day will help to create a sense of mental clarity that will allow you to better gauge your own emotional temperature and more easily feel in control of the physical symptoms that may accompany your anxious thoughts.

Many times when we panic we can feel as though we are an outside observer of what is actually happening. This type of panic creates derealization, a mental state where you feel detached from your surroundings. This occurs when the people and objects around you seem unreal but you are aware that this altered state isn't normal. The following technique will help you come back into the present moment.

THE TWO-MINUTE DESCRIPTION GAME

Notice what is around you and spend a few minutes taking in your surroundings and noting what you see. Using all of your senses, provide as much detail as you can to describe exactly what you see, what you hear, what you can feel, what you can smell, and what you taste.

Example:

> "The sweater I'm wearing is blue, but the shirt that man is wearing is red with black lettering. The bench I am sitting on is wood and is very smooth. My legs feel heavy and warm, since I am sitting in the sun. I can feel a warm breeze on my face, and it is blowing my hair. I notice the smell of grass being cut and children playing in the park in front of me. The grass looks green and brown. I can hear the children laughing."

List everyday activities that you do daily and describe them in detail. It can be as simple as taking a shower, chronicling your morning or evening routine, or cooking a meal.

Example:

> "When I woke up this morning, I turned off my alarm and then stretched my arms. I checked my phone and saw that I had a couple of new emails from work but did not answer any of them. I got out of bed and went into the bathroom to brush my teeth. After I brushed my teeth, I turned on the shower and got in. Once I was in the shower, I washed my body and then sham-

pooed my hair with a rose-scented shampoo. I got out of the shower and put lotion on my face. I went into the bedroom and picked out my red blouse and black pants for work. I brushed my wet hair and then blow-dried my hair."

On-the-Go Activity

Write description questions in your smartphone or on a piece of paper before you arrive at an environment that creates anxiety for you. Take this list with you whenever you are going to an environment that makes you anxious. Remind yourself that you can direct your thoughts back to the present moment at any time or in any place.

Healing Exercise

Describe your surroundings exactly where you are right now by answering the following questions:

- What do you see around you?
- What do you hear around you?
- What do you feel around you?
- What do you smell around you?
- What do you taste around you?

TWO-MINUTE HYDROTHERAPY

According to a 2006 study, bathing in cold water can reduce the cortisol hormone, which usually kicks into action when stress and anxiety take over.[1] Research has shown that acute cold exposure also can help to stimulate the vagus nerve. Cold-water immersion hydrotherapy can also lower your heart rate by up to 15 percent and increase endorphins, the feel-good hormones in the brain.[2] An example of cold-water immersion may be significantly lowering the temperature of the water in the shower for thirty seconds before getting out or running cold water on your hands for two minutes. This can act

---

1   M. Toda, K. Morimoto, S. Nagasawa, and K. Kitamura, "Change in Salivary Physiological Stress Markers by Spa Bathing," *Biomedical Research* 27, no. 1 (February 2006): 11–14, doi: 10.2220/biomedres.27.11.
2   A. Mooventhan and L. Nivethitha, "Scientific Evidence-Based Effects of Hydrotherapy on Various Systems of the Body," *North American Journal of Medical Sciences* 6, no. 5 (May 2014): 199–209, doi: 10.4103/1947-2714.132935.

as a mindfulness practice, which will help ground you in the present moment instead of worrying about future triggers that make you feel out of control.

How to Heal Using Hydrotherapy

1. Take a cold shower.
2. Splash cold water on your face.
3. Dip your feet in a cold-water bath.
4. If you are near a sink, run your hands under cold water for up to two minutes.
5. Fill a bowl of water with ice and submerge your face in it for fifteen seconds. Come up, breathe, take another deep breath, and submerge again. Repeat as often as you need until your nervous system has calmed. According to Happify.com, "This technique stimulates the 'dive reflex,' which is what happens when the body is submerged in freezing cold water and conserves energy to survive. Anxiety, at this point, is unnecessary and dissipates."[3]

On-the-Go Activity

Carry a stainless-steel water bottle filled with ice and/or water. If you feel yourself becoming anxious, take a couple of sips of water, splash some on your face, or even stick one finger at a time into the top of the bottle, count to five, and place your fingers on your cheeks for five seconds.

TWO-MINUTE CALMING MEDITATION

1. Take a deep breath in through your nose and out through your mouth. Repeat.
2. Allow your breath to return to normal, in and out through the nose. Pay attention to your breath and notice when your lungs expand.

---

3   Rachel Wells, "5 Ways to Stop Panic in Its Tracks," Happify Daily, https://www.happify.com/hd/5-ways-to-stop-panic-in-its-tracks/.

3. As you breathe, repeat the mantra "I am safe at this moment right now and I surrender to peace." (Healing tip: It may help to write this mantra on sticky notes and put them around your home.)

4. Follow the breath in as you feel your belly rise. Breathe out through your nose as you notice the breath leave your body, watching your belly fall.

5. What do you notice as you breathe? How does the air feel as it travels to the belly? What is the temperature of the air? Can you feel the air travel to the back of your throat?

6. After two minutes of conscious breathing, notice the change in your physical state and how you feel emotionally.

THE POWER OF AN "I" STATEMENT

It takes only a couple of minutes of the repetition of an "I" statement to send a calming message to your mind and body. Statements such as "I am safe, I am calm, I am peaceful" bring with them a peaceful feeling, which can help to reduce the production of cortisol and adrenaline that anxious thoughts create. There is actually healing happening in using these "I" statements, even when you are not feeling highly anxious! The more you adapt to this way of thinking, the more likely you will automatically re-cite these coping statements rather than focus on your irrational anxious thoughts.

Healing Exercise

Write five "I" statements that will help you through your healing journey.

1. _____

2. _____

3. _____

4. _____

5. _____

Write these statements on a Post-it and put them on your bathroom mirror, refrigerator, closet door (or any other places in your home where you can see them) and say them aloud multiple times a day. If you have a smartphone, enter these statements in your phone calendar or reminders and set an alert so you can see these statements multiple times a day.

TWO-MINUTE GROUNDING TOOL
USING YOUR FIVE SENSES

Wherever you are, if you are in a panic, chances are you may be experiencing derealization. This is when you feel so anxious that the people and objects around you may seem unreal. By using this technique, you are purposefully taking in the details of your surroundings by incorporating each of your senses and trying to notice small details that your mind would usually tune out. This grounding technique will help you feel more in control of your anxiety by turning your attention away from intrusive thoughts or worries and refocusing on the present moment.

Look Around You and Name

Five things you can see

Look around and bring your attention to five things you may not normally notice. Say the items aloud or in your mind.

Four things you can touch

Bring your awareness to four things you can touch around you such as the texture of your shirt, the surface of the chair you are sitting in, the smooth or rough consistency of your skin.

Three things you can hear

Listen closely to the sounds that surround you. What do you hear? It may be the wind, a TV show, the hum of a refrigerator, the noise of traffic, or people talking.

Two things you can smell
Notice smells in the air around you and look around for two things that have a scent (such as a candle, perfume, or freshly cut grass).

One thing you can taste
Carry gum, candy, or small snacks for this step. Pop one in your mouth and focus your attention closely on the flavor or flavors.

On-the-Go Exercise
Bring a calming item with you to environments that make you feel more anxious. Do you have a fidget toy that helps you? Maybe a beaded bracelet, a spinner, putty, essential oils, or anything you feel might bring you back to the present moment should you start to feel anxious. Use your sense of sight to describe the item in detail. What does the item look like? Colors? Shape? Texture?

TWO-MINUTE EFT TAPPING SOLUTION
What Is EFT?
Emotional Freedom Technique (EFT), also known as "tapping," is a holistic tool that, similarly to acupuncture, focuses on meridian points (or energy hot spots) to help restore balance to your body's energy. EFT is based on the premise that the body consists of energy fields and that imbalances in this system cause physical and emotional issues. Gary Craig, the founder of EFT, believed that this energy-based form of psychotherapy is designed to reduce symptoms of psychological distress by manipulating how energy flows in the body. When practiced consistently, EFT can help balance the body's energy system and eliminate most negative emotions within minutes.

Experts in the field hold that tapping helps you access your body's energy and sends signals to the part of the brain that controls stress. They further contend that stimulating the meridian points through EFT tapping can reduce the stress or negative emotion you feel, ultimately restoring balance to your disrupted energy.

Tapping works by stimulating the body's energy meridian points by tapping them continuously to relieve emotional problems, stress, chronic pain, addictions, phobias, post-traumatic stress disorder, and physical diseases. Based on Chinese medicine, meridian points are thought of as energy pathways that flow through the body and help balance your physical and mental health. Any imbalance can influence disease or sickness. While EFT healing is similar to acupuncture in principle, acupuncture uses needles to apply pressure to these energy points. EFT uses fingertip tapping to apply pressure. According to the Tapping Solution,

> During an EFT session, the individual will gently tap themselves at certain meridian points and in a prescribed sequence with their fingertips. While tapping, they focus on the thoughts, feelings, and physical sensations that they want to get rid of, such as focusing on their anxiety and tightness in their chest. EFT tapping therapy is a highly effective, noninvasive, healthy self-help alternative to long-term psychotherapy.[4]

When we are in a highly anxious state, our brain tricks us into believing we are in danger and our central nervous system becomes out of balance. EFT tapping increases focus to help reduce distress and has shown positive results when treating anxiety, trauma, phobias, panic, depression, addictions, and grief.

How to Practice EFT

1. Identify the problem:
   • Begin by identifying the issue by making a mental note of what problem you are facing at this moment. This will become the target at which you "aim" the EFT tapping. Examples might include an upset stomach or feeling anxious about an upcoming social gathering. Remember to target only one issue at a time.

---

4   "What Is Tapping and How Can I Start Using It?" Tapping Solution, accessed September 12, 2020, https://www.thetappingsolution.com/what-is-eft-tapping/.

2. Measure the level of intensity of the problem (0–10):
   - On a scale of 0–10 (with 10 being the worst or most difficult), measure your level of anxiety related to a current problem. This scale assesses the emotional or physical pain and discomfort you feel and serves as a benchmark to which we can compare our progress after each round of EFT tapping.
   - For example, if you start at an 8 prior to tapping and then eventually reach a 4, you know you have achieved a 50 percent improvement.
3. Begin with tapping the karate chop (KC) point with your index and middle fingers:
   - The KC point is on the outer edge of the hand, on the opposite side from the thumb.
4. While tapping the KC point, recite this phrase three times: "Even though I have this [fear or problem], I deeply and completely accept myself."
   - The [fear or problem] above represents the problem you want to address. Examples: Fear of snakes: "Even though I have this *fear of snakes*, I deeply and completely accept myself." Sadness about rejection from my breakup: "Even though I have this *sadness about my breakup*, I deeply and completely accept myself."
5. Now take a deep breath and get ready to begin the tapping sequence:
   - You can use all four fingers or just the first two (the index and middle fingers). Four fingers are generally used on the top of the head, the collarbone, under an arm, and in wider areas. For other areas, such as around the eyes, you can use just two.
   - Tap with your fingertips, not your fingernails.
   - Use firm but gentle pressure.

Karate Chop Point

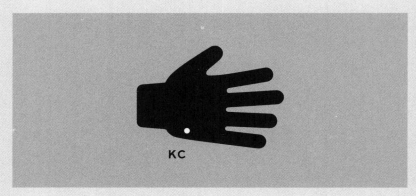

KC

Eight Body Tapping Points

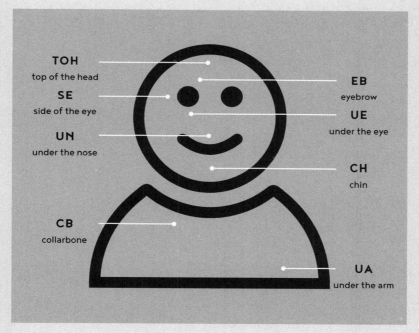

TOH
top of the head

SE
side of the eye

UN
under the nose

CB
collarbone

EB
eyebrow

UE
under the eye

CH
chin

UA
under the arm

6. Tap the following pressure points five to seven times in ascending order:
   - The tapping order begins at the top and works down. You can end by returning to the top of the head to complete the loop. Repeat the healing phrase you created in step 4 as you go through each point:
     1. Top of the head (TOH)
     2. Eyebrow (EB)
     3. Side of the eye (SE)
     4. Under the eye (UE)
     5. Under the nose (UN)
     6. Chin (CH)
     7. Beginning of the collarbone (CB)
     8. Under the arm (UA)

On-the-Go Activity

Search these keywords on your smartphone and watch a video to help you calm your nervous system in less than two minutes using EFT tapping. Many of the top search results for each should be examples at the moment.

- EFT tapping for anxiety
- Emotional freedom technique for anxiety
- EFT tapping for panic attacks
- How to use tapping to calm anxiety
- Tapping for overwhelm and stress
- How to stop anxiety fast using tapping
- Two-minute tapping technique
- Tapping therapy for phobias

GROUNDING YOURSELF BY SELF-SOOTHING

In chapter 2 we talked about grounding and why it is so important in the process of healing anxiety. Struggling with any mental illness can make it very difficult to stay in the present moment and can leave you feeling irritable, angry, panicky, frozen, or numb. These self-soothing grounding exercises will help train your brain on how to focus more on the present moment and less on intrusive, anxious thoughts about the future. Grounding tools are especially helpful to bring your mind and body back to a state of homeostasis (a healthy and stable internal state of being) and can help you focus more on the here and now.[5]

USING MUSIC TO HEAL ANXIETY

What is your favorite song and why? Think about it. Music can change our moods and make us feel like we're not alone. Music is healing, as it takes us back to a place and time that we remember fondly. It helps us express our feelings when sometimes words fall short. If you find it hard to verbally express your emotions, music can help you to find themes and meaning that apply to your life experiences. This can then help you to find the words that represent how you are feeling. Songs allow you to calm your nervous system, relax, and heal your soul. One study found that music therapy had positive effects on decreasing levels of depression and anxiety in patients with cancer and is now recommended in most nursing home facilities![6]

Exercise 1: Music to Match Your Mood

Rate anxiety 1–10: _____
Before Match Your Mood: _____
After Match Your Mood: _____

Begin by tuning into any negative emotions that are coming up for you right at this moment. Use the following space to write any negative feeling or feelings you are experiencing right now. Some examples include:

- Sad
- Mad
- Scared

---

5   Rachel M. Eddins, ed., "Grounding Techniques & Self Soothing for Emotional Regulation," Eddison Counseling, April 1, 2020, https://eddinscounseling.com/grounding-techniques-self-soothing-emotional-regulation/.
6   M. Jasemi, S. Aazami, and R. E. Zabihi, "The Effects of Music Therapy on Anxiety and Depression of Cancer Patients," *Indian Journal of Palliative Care* 22, no. 4 (October–December 2016): 455–58, doi: 10.4103/0973-1075.191823.

- Worried
- Jealous
- Frustrated
- Disgusted
- Lonely
- Annoyed

What other feelings do you experience? List them here:

_____

_____

_____

Now pick some songs that match the way you feel and list them here:

1. _____

2. _____

3. _____

4. _____

Now listen to these songs.

Time to elevate: What are some songs that can help to elevate your mood? Make a list of these songs on your smartphone or list them here:

1. _____

2. _____

3. _____

4. _____

Now listen to these songs. How do you feel after listening to songs that elevate your mood? Write about it here or in a journal.

_____

_____

_____

Exercise 2: Mindful Music Technique and Journaling

Rate anxiety 1–10: _____
Before Mindful Music _____
After Mindful Music _____

1. Pick a new song to listen to (choose a slower or more happy song).
   - Name a song you have never heard before. Really listen to the words. Do the words tell a story? What about?
2. Keep a music journal.
   - Another healing tool is a music journal, which can help to process and collect your negative thoughts and feelings. This may improve your focus on the here and now rather than the worry or pain. While listening to a song of your choice, write down any and all thoughts and emotions that come up for you at that moment.
3. Answer these questions.
   - What is it about that song that evokes the emotion or emotions you are feeling?
   - Does it make you feel like someone else can relate to your pain?
   - Does the song create a shift in your mind that helps you feel less alone?
   - What would you say to the person who wrote this song to help him or her feel better?
   - How could you help relieve his or her pain?
   - How do you think things might change if you responded to yourself in the same way that you typically respond to a close friend when they are suffering?

Play a song that you know every word to. Put the song on repeat, and as you listen to the song, write down the lyrics. This activity takes your mind off your anxious thought pattern and diverts your attention to a more important task.

Make a feel-good playlist filled with songs that make you feel happy and excited. Include songs that remind you of a happy memory or make you want to get up and dance. You may also want to make a calming playlist filled with quiet songs, instrumental slow songs, or meditative type of music.

TWO-MINUTE SELF-SOOTHING JOURNAL PROMPTS (EVEN FOR THE ANTIJOURNAL PERSON)

Journaling is one of the most effective tools when it comes to healing your anxiety. Think of writing as medicine for your mind. We have thousands of thoughts every day, which makes it hard to pinpoint what may be contributing to the debilitating anxiety some of us feel daily. It can feel paralyzing when intrusive thoughts become louder and louder and we often begin to feel mentally and emotionally exhausted. Writing and journaling the things that bother you will help you structure your thoughts and bring peace to your mind. When our mind is overflowing with fearful or irrational thoughts, it can almost feel like there is an internal traffic jam of anxiety! When you reach this point, you need a tool to bring some consistency and structure to your thoughts. The tool I'm speaking of is a simple piece of paper (and a pen).

Write, Don't Type

While you may prefer to use your phone or computer to journal, it is recommended that you use a pen and paper to write out your thoughts. This is because the act of writing is a more mindful exercise. Writing by hand forces you to slow down and actually increases activity in the brain's motor cortex, an effect that's similar to meditation.[7] This explains why journaling by hand can be more therapeutic and cathartic. Journaling by hand

---

7   Kristin Wong, "Journaling Showdown: Writing vs. Typing," Lifehacker, March 5, 2017, https://lifehacker .com/journaling-showdown-writing-vs-typing-1792942629.

can help you find true appreciation in the good things or the challenging things that may be happening in life. It also provides an outlet to help you really think things through.

The more you use your journal to rewrite your story, reframe your thinking patterns, and replace automatic negative thoughts, the more likely your healing will progress. This works because of something called neuroplasticity. Neuroplasticity is the "muscle-building" part of the brain that gives us the ability to respond to change and adapt by forming new neural pathways. With repeated and direct attention, we all can rewire our brain. New thoughts and skills carve out new pathways. The brain is always evolving and never stops changing in response to learning. Repetition and practice strengthen these pathways, forming new habits. This means that the more we practice exercising our brain, the stronger it becomes and what we don't practice fades away. So if we continuously write down the way we want to think and how we want to live, we can actually change our brain pathways. It takes consistent repetition to change these pathways but over time, it becomes automatic—we literally become what we think and do!

Rule 1: There Are No Rules

There are no rules when it comes to how to journal, but one suggestion is to begin by free associating. Free association is a term created by Sigmund Freud, the father of psychoanalysis, and he refers to this process as "discovering your genuine thoughts, memories, and feelings by freely sharing all the seemingly random thoughts that pass through your mind."[8] This means to just begin writing whatever comes to your mind. Don't worry about grammar, punctuation, or even completing full sentences. Just get out whatever thoughts are going through your mind at that time. Write about whatever is on your mind or whatever is bothering you. Try to keep going until you feel you have written what needs to be said, but not to the point of rumination. Also, remember not to judge yourself by what is coming out on paper. Acknowledge that what is coming out of your mind is 100 percent okay and that they are just thoughts and do not have any

---

8   Jon Jaehnig, "Free Association: What Is It, and How Does It Work?" Betterhelp, November 10, 2020, https://www.betterhelp.com/advice/psychologists/free-association-what-is-it-and-how-does-it-work/.

power over you. This can help you learn how to let go of situations that bother you and free your mind from distracting thoughts.

How to Start a Journal

1. **Start by getting something to write on.** It doesn't have to be one of those fancy spiral-bound journals with inspirational phrases such as "Today is the first day of the rest of your life" or something similar on the cover (but if that's your thing, more power to you). You can literally take an office notepad and just start writing. Or better yet, go to a dollar store and just buy one of those notebooks you used in grade school. All you need is paper and a pencil or pen.

2. **Set a timer.** A good way to start journaling is giving yourself a time limit of five to ten minutes to get your thoughts down on paper. If you leave it open-ended, it might start to seem daunting, or you may start to get bored. When you have a set time, you're more likely to focus, and you'll get more out of the time you spend writing.

3. **Schedule it.** If you have a busy calendar or struggle to prioritize journaling (and you know it is a coping tool that helps you), schedule journaling time into your daily routine. Remember, five to ten minutes daily are all you need. Look at your daily schedule and see when you are more likely to have time to write and when it will be most helpful. Try it for at least twenty-one days and watch it become a daily healing habit.

Journal Prompts

If you feel like having some prompts to follow is more effective for you, then don't worry—I got you! Anxiety can sometimes lead to feeling "stuck" inside your own head, which makes it difficult to know where to begin when it comes to journaling. Journal prompts act as therapeutic guidelines to tackle targeted emotions and can allow you to better express

52   THE ANXIETY HEALER'S GUIDE

yourself in a different way while becoming more aware of your anxious thought pattern.

The following journal prompts will give you some guidance on how to begin the journaling process and get the brain juices flowing. The first set of prompts are self-reflective and will help you gain more insight into your anxious thought patterns, limiting beliefs, and fears. The second set of journal prompts are healing. These prompts will aid in changing the false narrative you hold in your mind that may be contributing to your anxiety and holding you back from living your best life.

Bonus healing tip: Write for at least two minutes. Write longer if you feel compelled to do so.

Self-Reflective Prompts

- Rate how anxious you feel on a 1–10 scale. Does this number vary from day to day? Does this number vary from morning to night? Keep a log.
- What do you feel anxious about right now? Are these thoughts 100 percent true? Why or why not?
- How do you know that you're feeling stressed or anxious?
- What do you think your anxiety might be trying to tell you?
- Do you feel anxiety or tension in your body? If so, where in your body?
- How could you see your anxiety as helpful?
- What situations create anxiety for you? What aspects of these situations do you have the power to change?
- List anyone who makes you feel nervous or anxious when you're around them. What aspects of these people do you have the power to change?
- What thoughts, or "self-talk," tell you that you're anxious? (Review the list of cognitive distortions that was provided in the introduction.)
- What do you think is the worst thing that could happen? How likely do you think this is to happen?

- Imagine your best friend has the same anxiety as you. What would you say to that friend to help support him or her through it?
- Think of the last time you let negative thoughts spiral out of control. What were some of those thoughts?
- Write about the last time you cried. What caused you to cry?
- Write a letter to your inner child. What advice can you give him or her to better navigate his or her mental health? How could you nurture him or her?
- Write about a time when you were feeling anxious and it went away. What did you do to help yourself?
- What secrets are you keeping? Are these secrets affecting your mental health? Why or why not?
- If you weren't afraid, what are five things you would do? Can you think of any ways to overcome this fear?

Healing Prompts

- The last time I was anxious I felt better by . . .
- My happiest memory is . . .
- I can release negative energy in my life by . . .
- Five things that make me feel better after a bad day are . . .
- My perfect day would be . . .
- The three biggest obstacles I've overcome are . . .
- Three things that have helped when I felt stressed or anxious in the past are . . .
- Some coping skills I have to deal with my anxiety are . . .
  - When I use these coping skills . . .
  - My coping skills plan will be . . .
- Today I am thankful for these ten things . . .
- Ten accomplishments that I am proud of are . . .
- What I would tell my younger self to help better navigate my mental health is . . .

- What made me smile today was . . .
- Five moments I felt the happiest were . . .
- I feel the most calm when . . .
- Today I felt proud when . . .
- The most hilarious thing to happen today was . . .
- My happy place looks like . . .
- One thing I'm glad I learned today was . . .
- One beautiful thing I saw today was . . .
- I am grateful that during my childhood I was able to . . .
- Three people I can connect with right now to help me are . . .
- I am glad to live in my home because . . .
- My favorite person to talk to is . . .
- One thing that made my life easier today was . . .
- My favorite song is . . .
- I felt loved today when . . .
- Five things I love to do are . . .

Bonus Writing Exercise

- Write a letter of forgiveness to someone who has caused you pain.
- Write down all your coping mechanisms. Evaluate the ones that are the most helpful and the ones that are the most detrimental.
- Write a list of ten things you want to remember during highly stressful times. (Use this later if you're feeling down.)
- Write yourself a letter forgiving you for something that has happened in your past.

Can You Add to This List?

_____

_____

_____

_____

_____

THE TWO-MINUTE PROGRESSIVE MUSCLE RELAXATION (PMR) TECHNIQUE

Progressive Muscle Relaxation (PMR) is an anxiety-healing tool that uses a methodical approach in which an individual systematically constricts and releases various muscle groups to relieve physical stress and calm the anxious mind. PMR is considered a relaxation technique just like breathing exercises, visualization, and yoga. When anxious it is common to experience symptoms such as muscle pain, tension, and stiffness. PMR is an effective calming technique to use when experiencing a panic attack, as it helps to counteract the fight-or-flight response.[9]

How to Practice PMR

Rate your anxiety 1–10: _____
Before PMR: _____
After PMR: _____

Begin by sitting or lying in a comfortable position and inhale deeply through your nose, feeling your abdomen rise as you fill your diaphragm with air. Then slowly exhale from your mouth. Repeat three to five times.

Start by tensing each muscle group for eight seconds, but not to the point of strain. Pay close attention to how it feels, and then release the tension. Notice how the feeling of relaxation differs from the feeling of tension.

- Feet: Curl your toes tightly into your feet, then release them. Flex your feet, then let them relax.
- Thighs: Squeeze your thighs together tightly, then let them relax.
- Torso: Squeeze your abdomen tightly, then release the tension and let it fall.
- Back: Squeeze your shoulder blades together, then release them.

---

9   C. M. Luberto et al., "A Perspective on the Similarities and Differences Between Mindfulness and Relaxation," *Global Advances in Health and Medicine* 9 (January 2020): 1–13, doi: 10.1177/2164956120905597.

- Shoulders: Lift and squeeze your shoulders toward your ears, then let your shoulders drop.
- Arms: Make fists and squeeze your arms close to the side of your torso; release.
- Hands: Make a fist by curling your fingers into your palm, then relax your fingers.
- Face: Scrunch your facial features to the center of your face, then relax.
- Full body: Squeeze all muscles together, then release all tension.

Take a deep breath in through your nose and exhale for a count of 6 out through your mouth. Repeat as many times as you like.

On-the-Go Activity

You can practice PMR any time and anywhere. The best part is that no one will even know you are doing it. Create a plan to use this technique in the car, at a party, visiting the doctor, or anywhere you feel anxious. By tensing and relaxing the muscles throughout your body, you can achieve a powerful feeling of relaxation. Additionally, progressive muscle relaxation will help you spot anxiety by teaching you to recognize feelings of muscle tension.

Bonus healing tip: Practice PMR at least three times per week, even when you are not feeling anxious.

TWO-MINUTE BODY SCAN

According to psychology experts, a body scan is one of the most effective ways to begin a mindfulness meditation practice and has many mental and physical benefits, including reducing stress, increasing focus, and improving sleep. This exercise involves scanning the entire body as you pay attention to the bodily sensations in a gradual sequence from your feet to your head. The purpose of the body scan is to reconnect to your physical self without judgment. Take notice of the sensations in your body as you bring awareness to any aches, pains, tension, or general discomfort.

How to practice: Record this body scan in your own voice (or in someone else's voice that is calming and safe to you). Listen to the recording at least two to three times per week.

Rate your anxiety 1–10: _____
Before Body Scan: _____
After Body Scan: _____

Begin recording here:

Notice your body wherever you are and feel the weight of your body sitting on the chair or laying on the floor.
Take a deep breath in for a count of 5, bringing awareness to the body.
Take a deep breath out for a count of 7, releasing tension and embracing peace.
Close your eyes if that's comfortable for you.
Notice your feet and become aware of any sensations in your toes. The weight. The pressure. The heat.
Take a deep breath in for a count of 5, bringing awareness to the feet and toes.
Take a deep breath out for a count of 7, releasing tension and embracing peace.
Shift awareness to your legs. Become aware of any sensations in your legs, your knees, and your upper legs. Release tightness in the muscles. You are safe.
Take a deep breath in for a count of 5, bringing awareness to the legs.
Take a deep breath out for a count of 7, releasing tension and embracing peace.
Notice your belly and upper body. Notice any sensations in your back and allow it to be just as it is, without changing it or fixing it.

Take a deep breath in for a count of 5, bringing awareness to the belly, chest, and back.

Take a deep breath out for a count of 7, releasing tension and embracing peace.

Shift awareness to your hands. What do you notice? Are your hands tense or tight? See if you can allow them to soften.

Take a deep breath in for a count of 5, bringing awareness to your hands.

Take a deep breath out for a count of 7, releasing tension and embracing peace.

Notice your arms. Feel any sensation in your arms. Let your shoulders be soft. Send self-compassion to your arms.

Take a deep breath in for a count of 5, bringing awareness to your arms.

Take a deep breath out for a count of 7, releasing tension and embracing peace.

Shift awareness to your head, neck, and throat. Notice the calm of your neck and throat. Let them be soft. Relax. Soften your jaw. Let your face and facial muscles be soft.

Take a deep breath in for a count of 5, bringing awareness to your head, neck, and throat.

Take a deep breath out for a count of 7, releasing tension and embracing peace.

Notice your whole body at this moment. You are safe. You are here right now.

Take a deep breath in for a count of 5, bringing awareness to your body.

Take a deep breath out for a count of 7, releasing tension and embracing peace.

Be aware of your whole body as best you can, and when you're ready, you can open your eyes.

Optional Journal Prompts

My body feels _____.
What three things are you grateful for at this moment?

TWO MINUTES IN NATURE

In 2012, researchers in Japan studied the psychological impact of something they called "forest bathing," meaning spending time around trees. The results of the study found that "forest bathing" reduced anxiety, boosted the immune system, and amplified feelings of well-being. Researchers concluded that exposure to trees, whether in a city park or a country forest, is what gives you the health benefits—you just need regular contact. Scientists say that part of the reason for reduced anxiety is the phytoncide essential oil that the trees release.

On-the-Go Activity

The one thing we know is that nature, specifically trees, has a calming effect on the mind and body.

- Make it a daily goal to go outside for at least ten minutes.
- Find an area with trees and either take a short walk, meditate, write in a journal, or just breathe in the smell of nature.
- If the sun is out, look up to the sky and feel its warmth on your face.
- During your outdoor adventure, place your hand over your heart and repeat this mantra out loud or to yourself, "I have control over how I feel, and I choose to feel at peace." Repeat this at least three times.
- If it's in your practice, journal about your experience.

TWO-MINUTE TECHNIQUES TO ADD
TO MY HEALING TOOL KIT

_____

_____

_____

_____

_____

_____

_____

_____

_____

_____

CHAPTER 4

Soothe Your Anxiety Away

When life feels a bit too intense, it can be hard to know how to soothe yourself. In fact, many sensitive, empathic people were never instructed on how to self-soothe when they were children. Perhaps your caregivers didn't hold you and reassure you that everything was going to be okay. Or maybe you grew up with anxious caregivers who were limited in their own way of coping. Children, especially those who are more intrinsically sensitive, can absorb this and may unknowingly carry it around as adults.

When the mind races and the body begins to tense, it is fairly certain that anxiety is creeping up. Self-soothing activities are vital in these moments because our body's sympathetic nervous system is stimulating our stress response. When this happens, our body is in a very hypervigilant state and our mind makes us believe we are in danger, when in reality, we are not. Self-soothing exercises will help activate the parasympathetic nervous system (i.e., the "rest or digest" response) and return the mind and the body to a more restful state.

Holistic psychologist Dr. Nicole LePera describes proactive soothing methods as a conscious choice we must practice daily, especially if we were not modeled appropriate ways of dealing with adversity in childhood.[1]

---

1 Nicole LePera, *How to Do the Work: Recognize Your Patterns, Heal from Your Past, and Create Your Self* (London: Orion Spring, 2021), 230–41.

The goal of self-soothing is to help return your body to a balanced state using emotional consciousness and soothing exercises/items. You never want to depend on only one way to soothe yourself, as that limits your healing. Developing as much flexibility as possible will allow you to respond better to adversity, tolerate discomfort, and believe that you can deal with distressing situations.

HEALING IN ACTION

These self-soothing items can be used in highly stressful situations to help manage your anxiety. This chapter will help guide you toward discovering what tangible items work best for *you*. Remember, your healing tool kit may take a little while to create as you are becoming more and more aware of your own responses to worry, anger, sadness, and fear. My suggestion is to try as many of these tools as you can, see which ones work the best for you, and incorporate those into your daily travels.

Self-Soothing Portable Items

1. Activity books such as dot to dots, mazes, word searches, *I Spy*, or anything similar.
2. Adult coloring book.
3. A pinwheel, as watching it spin steadily can help you slow your breath should you start feeling your heart race.
4. Art supplies such as paper and crayons, markers, or paint.
5. Audiobook or podcast.
6. Audio or video meditations that create safety and calm.
7. Blowing bubbles, which can help with slowing down your breath.
8. Book of inspirational sayings, as they can help elevate your mood and calm you down.
9. Bubble wrap.
10. Calming technique cards. One example may be a notecard with some breathing techniques written on it; another card may have some muscle relaxation exercises written

on it. These can be reminders to keep calm and focused wherever you are. Once you find an anxiety-relieving technique that works well for you, write it on a card to remind you.

11. CBD oil, but please check with your doctor before using.
12. Chewing gum. One study found that people who chew gum had lower cortisol levels, reduced levels of stress and anxiety, and increased levels of alertness and performance. It is said that gum can also improve a negative mood and tends to improve blood flow in the brain.[2]
13. Cold towel. If you can, take a cold towel with you wherever you go and use it on your face when you're feeling anxious. The cold temperature helps to stimulate the vagus nerve and activate the parasympathetic nervous system. This will help to bring your body down to a calmer state. It can also just be a good distraction, and the cool sensation can be really helpful if you overheat from anxiety.[3]
14. Coping cards. Write your favorite coping statements on index cards or in your smartphone. For example, try phrases such as "I can handle this" or "The feeling will pass."
15. Essential oils such as lavender, bergamot, and frankincense, which are known to alleviate anxiety.
16. Eye mask.
17. Fidget spinner.
18. Funny videos from YouTube or a similar site.
19. Glitter jar, which can provide peaceful visualization stimulation.
20. Herbal vitamins or supplements for anxiety such as magnesium, GABA, passionflower, valerian root, licorice root, ashwagandha, robiola, omega-3 fatty acids,

2   A. Scholey et al., "Chewing Gum Alleviates Negative Mood and Reduces Cortisol During Acute Laboratory Psychological Stress," *Physiology & Behavior* 97, nos. 3–4 (June 2009): 304–12, doi: 10.1016/j.physbeh.2009.02.028.
3   M. Jungmann et al., "Effects of Cold Stimulation on Cardiac-Vagal Activation in Healthy Participants: Randomized Controlled Trial," *JMIR Formative Research* 2, no. 2 (October 2018): e10257, doi:10.2196/10257.

B vitamins, and L-theanine. Always check with your doctor before taking any supplements.

21. Herbal remedy drops or nasal spray.
22. Hot tea. Make sure to grab anxiety-healing flavors such as chamomile, peppermint, valerian root, lemon balm, lavender, passionflower, rose petal, and matcha.
23. Ice pack. The cold temperature can break through dissociative feelings that often happen when anxious and offers immediate relief from heightened cortisol levels.
24. Journal to write any negative thoughts or to do a brain dump. You can also use the journal to keep track of your most effective coping statements when anxious.
25. List of at least one safe person in your support system, their names, and contact information.
26. Lotion with a calming essential oil scent. Lotion scented with lavender can create a sense of peace and calm.
27. Magnetic fidget stones. These shiny fidget stones make a fun desk toy or pocket-size trinket that you can take anywhere. Excellent for calming and for a little stress relief at your desk, during meetings, while traveling, or for homework time.
28. Mini massager.
29. Music that makes you feel calm or drifts you away into happier memories.
30. Noise-canceling headphones.
31. Peppermint candy. Eating a peppermint candy or inhaling the scent of peppermint aromatherapy products may aid with fatigue and nausea. It may also help to bring you back into the present moment using your senses of taste and smell.
32. Pictures of people you feel safe with or pictures of a location that is calming for you or elicits happy memories.
34. Plastic snow globe. The visualization of the globe can help calm the mind.

35. Rubber band or bracelet to snap on wrist or to fidget with.
36. Rubik's Cube.
37. Scratch-and-sniff stickers. The sense of smell can bring you back to the present moment.
38. Shift breathing necklace. This necklace is designed to help you improve your breathing by slowing the exhalation (this helps to slow your heart rate). There is a small metal tube connected to the chain, and if you begin to feel short of breath, just breathe into the tube to slow your heart rate. The size of the opening and the two-flow airway are precisely designed to provide the ideal resistance for your exhalation.
39. Silly Putty.
40. Small bag of sand. Abstractly working with sand can be incredibly relaxing, and playing with sand works well to reduce anxiety because it increases mindfulness of the present moment, calms the mind, and reduces stress to help give yourself a break.
41. Squishy.
42. Stress ball.
43. Stuffed animal.
44. Water. Drink it slowly and focus on the sensations of taste, smell, and temperature.
45. Weighted blanket.
46. Word or number games, whether on your smartphone or on a small workbook, as they will distract your brain for the short term.
47. Worry stone. Worry stones are smooth, polished gemstones, usually in the shape of an oval with a thumb-size indentation, used for anxiety relief. This action of moving one's thumb back and forth across the stone can reduce stress.
48. Yarn for knitting or crocheting.

> **Disclaimer:** It is important to remember that essential oils are very potent, so you have to be cautious when you use them. Not everyone will respond to essential oils in the same way. The following information is educational only and does not replace medical advice.

Okay, you're probably thinking, *What is all the hype about essential oils these days?* Well, if you're feeling stressed, certain scents can help to lift your mood, feel more energized, and reduce stress and anxiety. Aromatherapy is a holistic healing treatment that uses natural plant extracts (essential oils) in a medicinal way. Studies have shown the effectiveness of the use of aromatherapy to help with pain management, stress relief, and even improving sleep.[4]

One study showed that aromatherapy helped intensive-care patients to feel less anxious and more positive immediately. This demonstrates how powerful our sense of smell can be when exposed to aromatherapy.[5]

Essential oils are absorbed into the body either through the pores of the skin or by inhalation through the nose. Because of their potency, it's important to use only a few drops of a diluted form of essential oils when applying them to the skin with a carrier oil such as coconut oil or vegetable oil. When stress or anxiety are related to everyday challenges, essential oils may be all that you need to find balance. Scientists believe that essential oils work by sending chemical messages to parts of the brain that affect mood and emotion. Although these scents alone won't take all your stress away, the aroma may help you relax. The essential oils that are known to relieve stress include lavender, chamo-

---

4   Jung T. Kim et al., "Evaluation of Aromatherapy in Treating Postoperative Pain: Pilot Study," *Pain Practice* 6, no. 4 (November 2006): 273–77.
5   Eun Hee Cho et al., "The Effects of Aromatherapy on Intensive Care Unit Patients' Stress and Sleep Quality: A Nonrandomized Controlled Trial," *Evidence-Based Complementary and Alternative Medicine* 2017 (December 2017): 2856592. doi:10.1155/2017/2856592.

mile, rosewater, bergamot orange, clary sage, lemon, neroli, rose, and ylang-ylang.[6]

Quality Check

It's important to look for a trusted producer that makes pure oils without anything added. Some more expensive oils may have vegetable oil added, which is completely normal. Look out for other additives, as you are more likely to have an allergic reaction to those added ingredients. According to Johns Hopkins University, "You're more likely to have a bad reaction if you have atopic dermatitis or a history of reactions to topical products. Because pure essential oils are potent, diluting them in a carrier oil (such as coconut oil or vegetable oil) is the best way to avoid a bad reaction when applying directly to the skin."[7]

While not common, if you experience irritation or allergic reactions (e.g., red, itchy rash or hives) after applying essential oils, see your doctor. Whether you're using your oils topically or aromatically, it is recommended to start slowly with one to two drops. You can always add another drop when you're ready. Remember, a little goes a long way! Do not put essential oils in eyes, ears, nose, or other areas with sensitive skin. You can apply essential oils to most parts of your body, but you want to be cautious of your most sensitive areas. You may find that application of oils may benefit certain areas more effectively than others.

Shopping for the Right Essentials Oils

Read the Label

A bottle of essential oil should clearly state the common and Latin names of the plant used to make the oil, list all of the ingredients in the formula, state the country in which the plant was grown, and specify that it is "100 percent pure essential oil." Avoid any label that says "essence oil" or "fragrance oil." These fake oils are made from essential oils combined with chemicals or entirely from chemicals. THAT IS A NO-NO! Look only for

---

6   Lorena R. Lizarraga-Valderrama, "Effects of Essential Oils on Central Nervous System: Focus on Mental Health," *Psychotherapy Research* 35, no. 2 (February 2021): 657–79.
7   "Aromatherapy: Do Essential Oils Really Work?" Johns Hopkins University, accessed September 20, 2020, https://www.hopkinsmedicine.org/health/wellness-and-prevention/aromatherapy-do-essential-oils -really-work.

bottles that contain a single essential oil in its purest form (100 percent essential oil with no fillers).

Evaluate the Company

Evaluating the company before you buy is vital because you want products that have a good reputation and have been around for at least several years. Find out if the supplier distills their own essential oils. The best oils are ones that are altered the least, which means no additional pressure or heat. This will ensure the most therapeutic value.

Check the Bottle

When looking to buy a pure essential oil, make sure the bottle is in a dark-colored (usually amber) glass bottle. The dark-colored bottle is helpful because light and heat can damage essential oils. The glass is vital because pure essential oils are highly concentrated and can dissolve plastic bottles over time, tainting the oil.

Compare Prices

Make sure to look at the prices of oils you are considering. Some pure oils are expensive, depending on the harvesting and production of the oils. Rose oils or sandalwood oils will be more expensive, while sweet orange oil will be on the less expensive end. If you find a more expensive pure oil for a cheap price, then it's most likely not the real thing.

Heal Using Aromatherapy

1. Put a small drop of lavender oil on your pillowcase to help you sleep better.
2. Apply an essential oil–scented lotion to your skin.
3. Put two to three drops of your favorite calming essential oil in about two cups of water and stir. Dip in a cotton washcloth, wring it out, and place it on your face and neck. Make sure to store the cloth in a sealed container in the refrigerator for later use.

4. Put one to two drops of essential oil on a cotton ball or fabric. Inhale the scent and allow calm to wash over you. You can add to the vents in your car, your gym bag, or on your pillowcase.

5. Put the oil in a diffuser! Diffusers disperse essential oils into the air and fills any area with the natural fragrance of your choice. One of the best ways to use a diffuser is during the night to help with sleep. Some diffusers last as long as twelve hours.

6. Aromatherapy accessories are another way to use aromatherapy throughout your day. There are necklaces, bracelets, and keychains made with special absorbent materials that you apply essential oils to and sniff throughout the day.

7. Take a few drops of your favorite essential oil into the palms of your hands. Cup your hands around your mouth and nose and inhale. Take three slow and deep breaths. Repeat as long as needed.

8. An aroma stick (or essential oil inhaler) is another way to inhale your favorite essential oil. These portable plastic sticks have an absorbent wick that soaks up essential oil and even comes with a cover to keep the scent fresh.

9. Use your favorite calming oil if you are receiving a massage. Many massage parlors and spas use essential oils to help create relaxation and a serene environment.

Other Essential Oils to Try

Try peppermint oil to boost mood and motivation. Additionally, citrus fragrances such as lemon have been known to help with moods and energy.

SOOTHING TECHNOLOGY TOOLS THAT HEAL

Learn all about the technology behind anxiety and what type of apps, videos, and various other social media outlets can be healing if you are struggling with anxiety. This section will provide anxiety-healing apps, social media experts, books, videos, online courses, and more that can help further your healing journey.

Top Mental Health Healing Apps

- 10 Percent Happier
- Anxiety Relief Hypnosis
- Aura
- Brain.fm
- Breath Ball
- Breathe+Simple Breath Trainer
- Breathe2Relax
- Breathe to Relax Pranayama App
- Breathly
- Breathwrk
- Breethe
- Buddhify
- Calm
- DARE
- Fabulous
- Fear tools
- HabitBull
- Happier
- Headspace
- HitomiNow
- iBreathe
- INSCAPE
- Insight Timer
- Kardia
- Liberate
- Mind Ease
- Mindshift CBT
- Moodfit

- MoodMission
- Moodnotes
- Moodtools
- MyStrength
- Nature Sounds Relax and Sleep
- Panic Relief
- Personal Zen
- Power of Calm
- PTSD Coach
- Rootd
- Sanvello
- Shine
- Simple Habit
- Simply Being
- Smiling Mind
- Steady
- Stop, Breathe & Think
- Streaks
- SuperBetter
- The Breathing App
- The Mindfulness App
- Wim Hof Method

Top Distraction Apps

- 1010!
- 2048
- Angry Birds
- Animal Restaurant
- AntiStress Anxiety Relief Game
- Candy Crush
- Colorfy
- Dots

- Elevate
- Geoguessr
- Homescapes
- Jigsaw Planet
- Lily's Garden
- Nonogram
- Pixel Art
- Simcity
- Six!
- Tetris
- Wordscapes
- Word Search Pro

ALISON'S TOP TWENTY-FIVE
ANXIETY-HEALING READS

These are some of my favorite anxiety-healing books that have in one way or another helped me in my own personal healing journey or with clients in my private practice. Some have been more helpful than others, but all have been effective in teaching me more about holistic healing at any stage of life.

1. *Anxiety: The Missing Stage of Grief: A Revolutionary Approach to Understanding and Healing the Impact of Loss* by Claire Bidwell Smith
2. *Anxiety Happens: 52 Ways to Find Peace of Mind* by John P. Forsyth, PhD, and Georg H. Eifert, PhD
3. *Be Calm: Proven Techniques to Stop Anxiety Now* by Jill Weber, PhD
4. *Dare: The New Way to End Anxiety and Stop Panic Attacks* by Barry McDonagh
5. *Dialectical Behavior Therapy Workbook: The 4 DBT Skills to Overcome Anxiety by Learning How to Manage Your Emotions* by David Lawson, PhD

6. *Don't Feed the Monkey Mind: How to Stop the Cycle of the Anxiety, Fear, and Worry* by Jennifer Shannon

7. *Feeling Better: CBT Workbook for Teens: Essential Skills and Activities to Help You Manage Moods, Boost Self-Esteem, and Conquer Anxiety* by Rachel Hutt, PhD

8. *Get Out of Your Head: Stopping the Spiral of Toxic Thoughts* by Jennie Allen

9. *How to Be Yourself: Quiet Your Inner Critic and Rise Above Social Anxiety* by Ellen Hendriksen

10. *How to Do the Work: Recognize Your Patterns, Heal from Your Past, and Create Your Self* by Dr. Nicole LePera

11. *Negative Self-Talk and How to Change It* by Shad Helmstetter, PhD

12. *Retrain Your Brain: Cognitive Behavioral Therapy in 7 Weeks: A Workbook for Managing Depression and Anxiety* by Seth J. Gillihan

13. *Rewire Your Anxious Brain: How to Use the Neuroscience of Fear to End Anxiety, Panic, and Worry* by Catherine M. Pittman

14. *The Anxiety and Phobia Workbook* by Edmund J. Bourne, PhD

15. *The Chemistry of Calm* by Henry Emmons

16. *The Highly Sensitive Person: How to Thrive When the World Overwhelms You* by Elaine N. Aron

17. *The Perfectionism Workbook: Proven Strategies to End Procrastination, Accept Yourself, and Achieve Your Goals* by Taylor Newendorp, MA, LCPC

18. *The Power of Now: A Guide to Spiritual Enlightenment* by Eckhart Tolle

19. *The Relaxation and Stress Reduction Workbook* by Martha Davis, Elizabeth Robbins Eshelman, and Matthew McKay

20. *The Stress-Proof Brain: Master Your Emotional Response to Stress Using Mindfulness and Neuroplasticity* by Melanie Greenberg

21. *The Wisdom of Anxiety: How Worry and Intrusive Thoughts Are Gifts to Help You Heal* by Sheryl Paul, MA

22. *Under Pressure: Confronting the Epidemic of Stress and Anxiety in Girls* by Lisa Damour, PhD

23. *When Panic Attacks: The New, Drug-Free Anxiety Therapy That Can Change Your Life* by David D. Burns, MD

24. *Widen the Window* by Elizabeth A. Stanley

25. *Worry Trick: How Your Brain Tricks You into Expecting the Worst and What You Can Do About It* by David A. Carbonell

MAKE YOUR OWN SELF-SOOTHING BOX

This box should consist of soothing tangible items that will be part of your anxiety-healing tool kit. I recommended having a range of sensory items that will help to focus your mind on something other than anxiety. You could include something to smell, something to touch, something to look at, and maybe even something to taste. It may be helpful to put miniature or travel-friendly items in the box, especially if you find traveling stressful or anxiety-provoking. Remember, this is *your* self-soothing box and is entirely personal to your needs.

Water

Water is healing for so many reasons, including helping reduce symptoms of panic. We all know that it is important to stay hydrated, but it's the coolness of water that can have a grounding effect. This can give you something to focus on when feeling anxious. The regular sipping is also a good way to keep a steady rhythm to your breathing. Keep a small cup or a small bottle of water in your self-soothing box as a gentle reminder to keep drinking.

Tangible Items to Touch

Tangible items serve as good distractions for your hands. This may include Silly Putty, fidget spinners, and stress balls. These items are satisfying to touch and encourage our muscles to relax. This can in turn reduce anxiety by activating the parasympathetic nervous system.

Items for Your Senses

Think of items you can add that will evoke the scent of smell. Consider putting some essential oils into your self-soothing box. Depending on what scents you prefer, some typical oils include peppermint for grounding, and lavender or rose for relaxation and tranquility. Another great item would be a candle. A candle is a perfect item to focus your sense of smell and can bring you back into the present moment. By consistently using these scents to help soothe yourself, you can end up associating the scents with relaxation, which may increase their effectiveness.

Positive Affirmation Cards

Create positive affirmation cards to put in your self-soothing box. It can be helpful to write your most healing affirmations down on a postcard, and when you begin to feel stressed or anxious, read your favorite statements aloud.

Supportive, Soothing Letters

Another self-soothing item that can create calm are letters or cards that you have received from friends and family. It can be really reassuring to see your positive attributes from the perspective of others written down. This can be super helpful if you are prone to feeling strong emotions about attachment and detachment of loved ones when struggling.

Quote Cards

Quote cards can be a great self-soothing item that can create a calm mind and body. Include your favorite uplifting quotes from films, books, poets, or accounts that you follow on social media.

Healing Books

Choose a couple of books from the preceding list or any others that have been most healing for you, and keep them in your soothing box. Make sure to complete any worksheets or read any pages that create calm when you need some extra self-soothing.

Memory Items

It may be helpful to include some photos of people or places that have only positive memories attached to them. These act as reminders of people you can turn to in times of struggle and that your life is made up of different elements, not just the anxious mind-set that you may find yourself in at that specific time. It may also help to remind you of how far you have come and how far you are capable of going in life. The simplicity of growing older and the progression of life may help reduce the pressure to constantly achieve and improve, which often helps with the initial feelings of anxiety or panic.

KEYWORD PHRASES TO SEARCH ONLINE FOR SELF-SOOTHING

Type these key phrases into Google to learn more about what type of self-soothing tools may work best for you!

- Self-soothing tools for anxiety
- Self-soothing tools for panic attacks
- How to self-soothe through an anxiety attack
- How to self-soothe through a panic attack
- Best soothing items for anxiety relief
- Soothing items for anxiety
- What is self-soothing?

SELF-SOOTHING ITEMS FOR MY TOOL KIT

_____

_____

_____

_____

_____

_____

_____

_____

_____

_____

_____

_____

_____

Part II

MIND TRICKS
TO EASE ANXIETY

CHAPTER 5

The Self-Talk Solution

THE INNER ROCK STAR EXERCISE

It's important to talk to yourself differently when you are in highly anxious situations. Everyone has an "inner rock star" that helps them through challenging situations, but many times that voice is silenced by our anxiety bully. It's time that we give our inner rock star a voice! And I mean that quite literally. This "inner rock star" exercise is compiled of five different healing scripts that you can read and record with your own voice (or a safe person's voice) and use as a guided meditation. You can listen while traveling, taking a walk, driving, or anytime you want some extra healing! This self-talk technique may help to redirect the anxious brain from a negative way of thinking to a more rational and positive state of mind . . . in any situation.

SCRIPTS

Following are some sample scripts that you can call on to help complete the exercise.

- "Body Relaxation"
- "The Breath"
- "The Here and Now"

- "Happy Place"
- "Morning Meditation"

"Body Relaxation"

Begin reading the relaxation script here:

Find a comfortable seated position and begin this meditation by taking a deep breath in through your nose, 2, 3, 4 . . . and out through your mouth 2, 3, 4 . . . take this time to close your eyes if you can and focus on your body sensations as you take another deep breath in 2, 3, 4 . . . and out 2, 3, 4 . . .

As your body begins to relax and the stress starts to float away, roll your shoulders forward . . . and then roll your shoulders back. Repeat this once more . . . roll your shoulders forward . . . and then roll your shoulders back.

Focus on your body sensations and take another deep breath in through your nose 2, 3, 4 . . . and out through your mouth 2, 3, 4 . . .

Next stretch your arms out and stretch your hands wide open and above your head. Spread your fingers wide and reach your arms high . . .

Now relax your hands and lower your arms . . .

Focus on your body sensations and take another deep breath in through your nose 2, 3, 4 . . . and out through your mouth 2, 3, 4 . . .

Now let your shoulders relax and lower your shoulders away from your ears . . .

Relax your jaw by dropping the lower jaw slightly . . . and remove your tongue from the top of your mouth. . . . Try to keep your top teeth from touching your bottom teeth.

As you fall into a state of tranquility, feel your body become still. . . . Take a deep breath in through your nose 2, 3, 4 . . . and out through your mouth 2, 3, 4 . . .

Repeat to yourself:

My body is safe right here . . . right now.
My body is safe right here . . . right now.
My body is safe right here . . . right now.
I am stronger than I think and will get through this.
I am stronger than I think and will get through this.
I am stronger than I think and will get through this.

Take a deep breath in 2, 3, 4 . . . and out 2, 3, 4 . . .

I believe in myself and I believe in my breath.
I believe in myself and I believe in my breath.
I believe in myself and I believe in my breath.
All will be well. You need this. Just breathe.
All will be well. You need this. Just breathe.
All will be well. You need this. Just breathe.

Just feel the stillness and peace of this moment. Right now . . . my
body is love . . . my body is at peace . . . my body is at rest. . . .
Take one more deep breath in through your nose 2, 3, 4 . . . and
out through your mouth 2, 3, 4 . . .

"The Breath"

Begin reading the relaxation script here:

Right now, take a second and welcome yourself into this moment
and be in the here and now. . . . Congratulate yourself for taking
the time to be present and wander into a peaceful and safe space
inside your mind.

Begin by checking in with yourself and finding your breath.
Take a deep breath in through your nose for a count of 4, hold
for 2, and breath out through your mouth for a count of 7. Feel

any sensations and any tightness in the body, as well as feeling of your mood. Feel your emotions and acknowledge whatever is being felt and let it just be. Whatever it is you are feeling at this very moment is valid. You are safe within these feelings. Find awareness and acknowledge whatever is to be felt.

Now bring your attention to the breath. Be mindful of your breath as the abdomen expands as you inhale and falls as you exhale. You are safe at this moment. You are alive and breathing at this moment. Take a slow breath in through your nose for 4, and out through your mouth for 7. As you breathe normally and naturally, feel the rise and fall of your stomach. You are safe at this moment. Your heart is slowing and finding peace and comfort at this moment. If your mind has wandered off, just compassion-ately and gently make a note of it "wandering" and then come back to the breath.

As you begin to get deeper into the stillness of the body and mind, you may experience some anxious thoughts, worries, or fears. . . . Just remember, they are just thoughts, worries, or fears and cannot hurt you. You are safe right at this moment . . . right now.

Choose to slow down and focus on your breath. . . . Take one inhalation in and one exhalation out at a time. Now focus on the body and tap into the sensations, thoughts, and emotions you are experiencing. Whatever you're feeling in the body and the mind, acknowledge what is being felt and just let it be.

Simply follow my voice, and if thoughts come up from time to time, do not worry, simply return to the breath. Allow yourself to become steady and calm. Find relaxation in the whole body. Focus on the body and become aware of the importance of total stillness.

As you breathe in through your nose and out through your mouth, focus your awareness on the motions of your stomach. Concentrate on your stomach as it gently rises and falls. With every breath, feel your stomach expand, breathing in . . . and breathing out.

Now bring the focus to your chest. With every breath you take, become aware of the chest gently rising and falling. Concentrate on the breath and continue to allow yourself to be at peace.

As we learn to be with things as they are, we can discover that our fears are truly just a figment of what is. Right now, at this moment, nothing can hurt you. You are right where you are supposed to be.

"The Here and Now"

Begin reading the relaxation script here:

Begin this meditation by taking three deep breaths in through your nose . . . and out through your mouth . . .

Inhaling . . . 1, 2, 3, 4
Exhaling . . . 1, 2, 3, 4
Inhaling . . . 1, 2, 3, 4
Exhaling . . . 1, 2, 3, 4
Inhaling . . . 1, 2, 3, 4
Exhaling . . . 1, 2, 3, 4

Look around and begin using your sense of sight to focus on five things you can see. What are three different shapes you notice? Look around you and describe the colors you notice.

Next . . . find four things around you that you can touch. What do you notice about the texture of what you can touch? Run your fingertips gently up the inside of your arm.

Feel the air across your skin. Walk barefoot on the grass and notice how your feet feel. Bring awareness to your clothing and how it is resting on your body. What is the texture of your pants and shirt? Hot, cold, sharp, hard, soft—there are many textures to experience.

Continue as you take a deep breath in . . . 2, 3, 4 . . . and out . . . 2, 3, 4.

Now close your eyes if you can and listen for three things you can hear. This can be any type of external sound. Maybe you hear cars driving by, your stomach growling, the wind blowing, or people talking. Whatever you hear, focus on three things that you can hear outside of your body.

Take another deep breath in . . . and a long sigh out through your mouth.

Now focus on your sense of smell and describe two things you can smell. It is okay if you need to take a walk to find a scent. Maybe you can smell a candle burning, soap in your bathroom, clothes from the washer, or the outside air.

Turn to your sense of taste. What is one thing you notice about the taste in your mouth? What does the inside of your mouth taste like? Gum, mint, coffee, or another flavor? If you have it available, find something small, such as a piece of chocolate or fruit, and really focus on the taste. Is it sweet, sour, or bitter? Just simply notice how your taste buds respond.

As you take a deep breath in . . . 2, 3, 4 . . . and out . . . 2, 3, 4 . . . remind yourself that you are safe right now . . . at this moment. You are alive and you are breathing.

"Happy Place"

Begin reading the relaxation script here:

Begin this meditation by taking a deep breath in through your nose for a count of 4 and out through your mouth for a count of 7. Become aware of your thoughts and watch them as they come in, then observe the thoughts as you just let them go . . . your body is becoming relaxed, and your breath is becoming slower and calmer.

All you need to do right at this moment is breathe and

listen . . . just breathe and listen . . . Focus on your breath as you breathe in and your stomach rises and as you exhale, your stomach falls, deep and relaxed. . . . Feel your body relaxing deeper and deeper, and allow your thoughts to just slow down. . . . Your limbs become limp, and your mind is calm. . . .

Now if you can, close your eyes. . . . If you are unable to do so, that is totally okay . . . just notice your breath and take another deep breath in through your nose for 4, hold for 3, and breath out through your mouth for 7. . . . Allow yourself to relax completely.

Now as you continue to breathe, use your imagination and picture a happy scene in your mind. . . . Visualize yourself at this "happy place." This could be somewhere you have been before, or someplace that you create in your mind. . . . This is a place full of inner peace and calm . . . and completely anxiety-free. . . . Just visualize it and imagine it as you breathe and listen.

Allow that breath deep into your belly, and let your stomach rise up as you breathe in and fall as you release your breath.

And picture yourself in your happy place, a warm and comforting setting that makes you smile. You are surrounded by all of the things that create so much joy and peace in your life. Take a few moments and create this scene in your mind. What do you see? What colors do you notice? Who is there with you in this place? Maybe it is just you, and that is just wonderful.

Visualize that place and see it very clearly in your mind. It is a wonderful place, isn't it? You are happy. You are healthy. You are safe.

Take another deep breath in and as you exhale allow yourself to feel even more comfortable and relaxed. . . . Take another slow breath in for 4 . . . and as you exhale, allow yourself to feel the joy and peace of your happy place. Allow yourself to feel completely relaxed. Completely at peace. Completely surrendering. Notice that you are in a safe place with no anxiety . . . and nothing can hurt you.

Now really see this place . . . commit to this memory. Think of every detail. Remember that in the future when you begin to feel anxious, you can just close your eyes, take a deep breath, and allow yourself to smile and remember this anxiety-free happy place that you have created for yourself.

Now as you hold on to the feeling of peace and joy, take a deep breath in . . . and as you exhale, listen to the sound of your breath . . . in and out . . . remind yourself that you are safe at this moment and you are secure in your special place. Anxiety does not live here any longer. . . .

When you are ready, simply start wiggling your toes and fingers . . . slowly open your eyes, smile, and just stay with your breath. . . .

Check in with yourself. . . . How are you feeling? Think of this happy place any time you begin to experience anxiety and use this meditation any time you want to experience full relaxation. Listen and breathe. . . .

Enjoy your day. . . .

"Morning Meditation"

Begin reading the relaxation script here:

As you open your eyes today, take a moment to inhale the new energy and exhale the old. Take the time to refresh, even if you are not fully awake yet. Today is a new day full of new possibilities.

Every morning that you wake is a morning that you get to choose how you want to go about your day. . . . You get to choose your mind-set today. . . .

This morning might be full of challenges, life is full of adversities . . . but you can overcome them. . . .

Right now I want you to check in with yourself and listen as you take a deep breath.

If you find yourself engaging in judgmental thoughts toward

yourself or others, notice ways in which you can release those judgments by transforming them into validating statements.

If you find yourself engaging in thoughts such as *I'm such a failure*, transform that thought with self-validation by thinking or stating aloud, "Progress and change take time and practice. I choose to be patient and direct compassion toward myself right now."

Give your mind and body the reassurance that you are on the right path toward a healing journey. Trust that what is best for you is coming to you. Know that your life is full of possibilities and be mindful that your thoughts, choices, and actions will play parts in crafting the kind of day that you want and deserve . . . even when frustrating moments occur.

As you start your day, think of everything you are grateful for. Take a deep breath and focus on three things you are grateful for at this moment. Gratitude creates joy and peace of mind. What three things bring you comfort? What three things bring you peace? What three things bring you a place of safety?

Take a deep breath in . . . 2, 3, 4 . . . and out . . . 2, 3, 4 . . .

Today is a new day, and a new day brings new possibilities. Ask yourself, *How do I want to feel today? How do I want to make the most of today?* Repeat this to yourself: *As I begin this new day, I am reminded that I am in control.*

Take a deep breath in . . . 2, 3, 4 . . . and out . . . 2, 3, 4 . . .

As you focus on your breathing, set an intention for the day by completing this statement: "I intend to . . ." Maybe it is an intention to love more, let go, sit with stillness, or just to be.

As you begin this brand-new day, think of all that you choose to let go of. What can you choose today to let go of? Is it feelings of unworthiness? Worry? Doubt? Anger? Guilt?

Whatever you choose, remember that you are on your own side, and you are worthy of love today. You are in control of today.

BREAK FREE FROM NEGATIVITY:
USING SELF-TALK TO BREAK THE NEGATIVITY LOOP

Struggling with anxiety means there is a chance that you struggle with intrusive negative thinking patterns. This negativity loop can feel paralyzing and constant. Many times this type of thought pattern is linked to hypercritical self-talk, which leads to chronic stress and over time may put us at risk for mental and physical disease. Our inner critic can create false beliefs about ourselves that influence self-esteem, confidence, and the quality of our relationships. This type of negative self-talk can act as a form of self-punishment in which we believe we are useless, stupid, worthless, and a failure. For some reason we feel it is 100 percent okay to talk to ourselves this way but would never think of talking to a friend or loved one in this manner.

So how do we break this negative loop? First you must work on recognizing the negative self-talk that consumes your mind. Then analyze these thoughts in a rational way and replace them with healthier and more accurate thinking. Remember, it is not easy to do all of this work on your own. As always, if anxiety is affecting your daily functioning, please seek help from a therapist in your area.

SELF-TALK TECHNIQUES
Affirmations

An affirmation is a short, powerful statement that allows you to consciously be in control of your thoughts. A lot of what we normally say and think about ourselves can be negative, which does not create good experiences for us. To truly change our lives and heal, we have to work on retraining our thinking and speaking in positive patterns. An affirmation is a statement that is carefully constructed to impact our daily lifestyle. When you say affirmations or think them, they become thoughts that shape your reality. Research shows that we have about sixty-two hundred conscious thoughts a day, and if you struggle with anxiety, there is a pretty good chance many of them are negative.[1] One of the tendencies of the mind is

---

1   J. Tseng and J. Poppenk, "Brain Meta-State Transitions Demarcate Thoughts Across Task Contexts Exposing the Mental Noise of Trait Neuroticism," *Nature Communications* 11 (July 2020): 3480, https://doi.org/10.1038/s41467-020-17255-9.

to focus on the negative and "play the same songs" over and over again. Being able to consciously think in a more positive way can make it easier to control the negative thoughts that are always threatening to take over.

Louise Hay, one of the most influential healers and pioneers of affirmation work, has dedicated her life to teaching others how to use affirmations to heal. Hay states, "An affirmation opens the door. It's a beginning point on the path to change by consciously choosing words that will either help eliminate something from your life or help create something new in your life."[2]

When actively using affirmations you are telling your subconscious mind, *I am taking responsibility and I am aware that there is something I can do to change.* Every thought you think and every word you speak are affirmations. All of our self-talk, our internal dialogue, is a stream of affirmations. You're affirming and creating your life experiences with every word and thought.

Remember, what you think, you believe. Your beliefs stem from habitual thinking patterns that you may have learned as a child, which could very well serve you in a positive or negative way. Negative thinking patterns may be limiting your ability to create the very things you say you want. Affirmations help you to pay attention to your thoughts more closely and begin to eliminate the ones creating experiences you do not want in your life.

When to Use Affirmations

There is no right or wrong time to use affirmations, but some experts say that there may be a greater benefit to using them in the morning.[3] Using affirmations in the morning gives you an opportunity to effectively start your day in a positive frame of mind. Morning affirmations may also help to shake off any negativity and keep your brain from filling up with any difficulties you may be facing. It is important to continue using affirmations consistently throughout the day to maintain that way of thinking. One way to create an effective affirmation practice is to write

---

2   Louise Hay, *Experience Your Good Now!: Learning to Use Affirmations* (Carlsbad, CA: Hay House, 2010).
3   Sally Kirchell, "10 Benefits of Starting Your Day with Positive Affirmations," Elephant Journal, November 28, 2018, https://www.elephantjournal.com/2018/11/10-benefits-of-starting-your-day-with-positive-affirmations-2/.

these statements on an index card or sticky note and keep them in a place where you can consistently see them (e.g., bathroom mirror, light switch, refrigerator).

How to Make Affirmations Successful

1. Write your affirmations using the present tense. Write affirmations about your life as if you already have what you want. This helps your mind to visualize the outcome. For example, you can say "I have an abundant life filled with love and joy" instead of "I will find love from others and create joy."
2. Keep it a simple statement. You are more likely to remember a self-talk statement that is short and sweet.
3. Use no negative words, only positive ones. Do not use negatives in your affirmation. Instead of saying "I will not say mean words to myself" say "I accept myself for all that I am and that is worthy."
4. Make it mean something. Make sure your affirmation means something to you. Make sure affirmations speak to you and are meaningful on all levels.

Following are some examples of affirmations that may be helpful in certain environments that have shown to create some anxious thinking patterns when outside of the home.

Basic Calming Self-Talk

Much of what we say to ourselves when experiencing anxiety in fact causes us to feel more anxious. Tell yourself calming phrases such as:

"This feeling will pass."
"I will get through this."
"I am safe right now."
"I am feeling anxious now, but soon I will be calm."
"I can feel my heart rate gradually slowing down."

Restaurants

I am safe at this moment.

This feeling is temporary . . . it will pass.

I am allowed to take as much time as I need to eat, and others will understand.

I can do difficult things that my anxiety tells me I can't.

You are at your own table and you are in control.

If you need to use the bathroom, it is right over there.

I can choose to focus on the food I'm eating and the company I am with.

Relax and remember you are doing great.

I'm stronger than I think.

I can feel anxious and still deal with this.

I am not attached to this restaurant. If I need to get fresh air, I can go outside and breathe.

I can handle this one step at a time.

Doctor's Offices

I choose to be here. Whatever the outcome, I am strong enough to get through it.

In this moment I am safe and have strength.

I have survived before, and I will survive now.

I am stronger than I think and will get through this.

It is okay to feel nervous about the doctor. It is a normal reaction.

I believe in myself and I believe in my breath.

All will be well. You need this. Just breathe.

The doctor is here to help me. This is not dangerous.

I can do difficult things that my anxiety tells me I can't.
If anything were to happen, I am in the best place.

Cars

I am trusting this car ride and believe I will get to my destination.
This won't last forever.
I can do difficult things that my anxiety tells me I can't.
It will be over soon and I will be safe.
I am allowed to pull over if I feel overwhelmed.
Anxiety is uncomfortable, but it is not dangerous. I will treat it with kindness. I got this!
I can listen to my favorite song or podcast while in the car to help me find balance.
Right now, at this moment, I am okay.
If I miss this turn, I can just turn around and take my time.
I can talk to other cars as if they were people. "Oh, hello blue car! I didn't see you there. Go right ahead in front of me."
I am not in danger. Soon I will arrive at the place I want to be.

Social Events

I have permission to leave the room or take a break if I feel uncomfortable.
I am kind and open. I will focus on connecting and not correcting.
I am safe and no one can hurt me.
I've got this. I can get through this and I will feel better after I do.
This is all temporary.
I can feel my breath and take a bathroom break if I need to.

I am safe and loved.

Everyone here is probably thinking about themselves, not me.

I am not alone. There are other people here just like me.

People here are not looking at me. I can just relax and be my amazing self.

It is okay to feel this way. My feelings are valid, but they do not control me.

Family Events

I am in control, and this feeling is temporary. I am okay.

Being with family is not comfortable, but I can handle it.

I can feel anxious and still deal with this situation.

Just breathe. I can do this.

I am calm, I am safe.

I breathe in calm and relaxation and breath out fear.

My family does not define me. I am worthy.

I am unique, beautiful, and important. I am enough.

I am doing the best I can.

Stop and breathe. I can do these.

Work

This seems overwhelming now, but I will be okay and will have some alone time soon.

I got this. Just remember to breathe.

This job is not the only one for me.

I am human and I am allowed to worry about work.

This feeling is not going to last forever.

My thoughts are just thoughts. They do not have power!

If I have to, I can excuse myself to go to the bathroom and take some deep breaths.

Remember that done is better than perfect.

I am safe. Nothing is going to hurt me.

I am capable. I am enough. I can make mistakes and still be good enough.

This is not the first time I've felt this way . . . remember, it will pass.

Grocery Stores

Right now I am not in danger. Right now I am safe.

I know the items I need and can get through this.

My thoughts are just thoughts. They are not always true or factual.

I will learn from this experience, even if it seems hard to understand right now.

This is difficult and uncomfortable, but it is only temporary.

I can choose to see this challenge as an opportunity.

I can always use my coping skills and get through this.

Nighttime

Tomorrow is a new day full of new chances.

I am safe in my bed at this moment right now.

My worries today will not change the outcome of what will be.

These are just thoughts that are trying to scare me . . . they do not have any power.

This will pass, as it always does.

Remember to breathe.

I can always listen to a sleep story or a podcast to distract my brain.

Morning will come and I can begin again.

I am loved.

I made it through the day and tomorrow is a new day.

I am safe. I am restful. I will rest to feel my best.

I will think of my happy place or my favorite memory and describe it in detail.

It will be okay if I don't sleep much tonight. Tomorrow night is another chance.

Bonus Healing Activity

Write down the affirmations that are most helpful for you below.

1. _____

2. _____

3. _____

4. _____

5. _____

On-the-Go Activity

Write your favorite affirmations on a notecard to take with you or save them in your phone. Look at this list any time you begin to feel overwhelmed to remind yourself, and your brain, that you got this!

CHANGING YOUR NEGATIVE SELF-TALK

Negative self-talk or self-limiting statements can be very damaging and can lead to feeling more stressed and helpless. This type of negative self-talk can lead to intrusive "what if" thoughts and fears of what "could happen." This type of internal dialogue is also known as our inner critic, which is a little voice inside that says "I can't handle this!" or "This is impossible!" Self-limiting statements are particularly damaging because they increase your likelihood of depression and increase stress in any given situation. So how can we work to change this habit? Keep reading to find out!

1. Recognize when you are having a negative or unhelpful thought.

2. Engage in "thought stopping."
   - Say aloud "STOP" when you are having an irrational thought and tell yourself that a thought is just a thought. It does *not* have power.
3. Ask yourself these questions:
   - Is this thought true? What evidence do I have that what I'm thinking is really true? What is the evidence against it?
   - Is this thought helpful? Can I think of a more rational thought?
   - What would I tell a friend in this situation?
   - Is there another way of looking at this situation? What are some other points of view?
   - What is the worst-case scenario? What is the most likely outcome? If the worst did happen, how could I cope?
   - What coping tools can I use right now to help shift my mind-set?
4. Work on changing the negative messages you are saying to yourself to morerealistic ones to bring about more pleasant and helpful emotions.

Affirmations

YOUR TOP FIVE HEALING AFFIRMATIONS

1.

2.

3.

4.

5.

Anxious Situation

Negative Self-Talk Statements

Coping Thought/ Realistic Statements

MIRROR WORK

Louise Hay states,

> The mirror reflects back to you the feelings you have about your-
> self. It makes you immediately aware of where you are resisting and
> where you are open and flowing. It clearly shows you what thoughts
> you will need to change if you want to have a joyous, fulfilling life.[4]

In other words, there is no hiding when you're in front of the mirror.
When we are in front of the mirror, we catch an intimate (and sometimes

---

4   Louise Hay, "What Is Mirror Work?" https://www.louisehay.com/what-is-mirror-work/.

painful) glimpse into the relationship we have with ourselves. Hay says that by looking at yourself in front of the mirror, while gently talking to yourself, you become more in touch with the inner self and develop more self-love, self-care, and a more compassionate and forgiving connection with yourself. Mirror work may feel awkward or uncomfortable at first, but it is one of the most effective healing methods I've found for learning to love yourself and see the world as a safe and loving place.

THE MIRROR EXERCISE

Mirror work brings our inner critic to the surface, but that is okay. By learning more about this inner critic, you can begin to shift your negative thinking patterns and begin using affirming self-statements to kick that critic in the butt and recognize the amazing person that you are! When we use affirmations with mirror work, we rewire the limiting beliefs that may have been creating a low self-worth.

Technique Tips

- Try to do this exercise in private so that you are not disturbed.
- Try to dedicate at least five minutes a day to mirror work.
- Use affirmations that feel true to you. (Even if only 1 percent of you believes it . . . USE IT!)

Mirror Exercise

1. Sit or stand in front of the mirror in your house for two to five minutes.
2. Look at yourself in the eye and don't look away.
3. What type of emotions come up for you? You may feel awkward, unsettled, embarrassed, emotional . . . you may feel some critical thoughts arise. Why? Because of that inner critic . . . but *stick with it*! It's okay to feel emotional—let yourself feel whatever comes up.

4. After five minutes, write in a journal any thoughts or emotions that come up for you. Were there any notable experiences?

5. As you continue to do your mirror work, it may help to process these emotions with a therapist.

Bonus Healing Activity

Practice saying these statements to yourself in the mirror every day:

- I'm so proud of you.
- I accept all that you are.
- I am beautiful.
- I support you.
- I completely trust you.
- I deserve love.
- I am enough.
- I love you.
- I appreciate you.

MIRROR WORK SCHEDULE

Practicing mirror work daily is one of the most healing steps you can take to live a life of self-love and inner peace. Place a checkmark in the box every time you complete mirror work!

Mirror Work Schedule

	Morning	Midday	Evening
Sunday			
Monday			
Tuesday			
Wednesday			
Thursday			
Friday			
Saturday			

CHAPTER 6

Visualization: Find Control by Using Your Imagination

Visualization is another powerful tool that can help activate the parasympathetic nervous system and relieve stress. Visualization uses mental imagery techniques that can help you relieve stress and achieve a more relaxed state of mind. When you are anxious or in a panicked state, your thoughts may wander, and you may tend to focus on the worry or worst-case scenarios. This only fuels our sense of fearfulness. Visualization exercises can help to expand your ability to rest and relax by focusing your mind on more calming and serene images. Similar to daydreaming, visualization is accomplished through the use of your imagination.

HOW DOES VISUALIZATION HEAL ANXIETY?

When you experience panic, your thoughts wander, and your mind may focus only on what is worrying you at that moment. Your mind clings onto the worst-case scenarios, jumps to conclusions, and focuses only on the negative outcomes. This adds to your sense of fearfulness. When practicing visualization, your brain shifts to a more rested and relaxed state by focusing on more calming and serene images. Visualization techniques can be thought of as a form of guided meditation or guided imagery.

Guided imagery is an element of distraction that helps to redirect people's attention away from what may be stressing them at the moment and toward an alternative focus. It is essentially a nonverbal suggestion provided to the body and subconscious mind to envision as though that peaceful, safe, and relaxing environment were real. These scenes then become a learned cue when beginning to feel anxiety creep in; thus, you recall memories and sensations from past guided imagery relaxation practices.

One of the main goals of a guided imagery practice is to help people learn how to detach from their obsessive minds and instead cultivate a relaxed image that is easy to watch. Guided imagery is a type of focused relaxation or meditation that involves intentionally thinking of a peaceful place or scenario and concentrating on the specific details to calm the mind.

When you think about a stressful or fearful situation, your body and mind become tense, your heart rate might increase, and you may feel jittery and out of control. If you focus your attention more on pleasant scenarios, your mind and body tend to relax. You may feel less tension in your muscles, and your mind will feel calmer and more at ease.

Guided imagery allows your mind to focus on the present and uses your imagination to help you cope better with stress and anxiety. We know that our thoughts affect the way we feel, which can in turn greatly alter our well-being. Studies have shown that visualizing positive and safe images during adversity can not only improve our ability to handle stress but may even improve our physical health, specifically irritable bowel disease.[1]

HEALING IN ACTION

Let's take a "mental vacation." It's time to relax, unwind, and briefly escape from our day-to-day tasks. This means that it is time to reshape our thinking patterns and create new pathways in our brain. Research shows that you can in fact rewire your brain because of its neural plasticity, also

1   Maya C. Mizrahi et al., "Effects of Guided Imagery with Relaxation Training on Anxiety and Quality of Life Among Patients with Inflammatory Bowel Disease," *Psychology & Health* 27, no. 12 (May 2012): 1463–79, doi:10.1080/08870446.2012.691169.

known as neuroplasticity.[2] This means that new neural pathways can be created in the brain by practicing mind exercises that help strengthen healthy habits such as visualization exercises. Visualization includes feeding pleasant images and stories into your subconscious mind, resulting in less anxiety. What happens is that instead of your anxious mind just naturally wandering wherever it wants to, you actively focus your attention on the relaxing images in your mind. If you train your brain to focus on past positive experiences and repeatedly visualize calming environments, then you can strengthen those neural pathways and weaken the others. After a few days you may begin to feel relief because your mental practice is now becoming a healthy daily habit. Try to spend ten to fifteen minutes per day on a preferred visualization relaxation exercise.

VISUALIZATION SCRIPTS

Similar to the "inner rock star" exercise in chapter 5, this visualization exercise is meant to be recorded in your own voice (or by someone you feel safe with who has a calming voice) and used as a guided imagery exercise. You can listen to this visualization recording while traveling, taking a walk, driving, or any time you want some extra healing! Studies show that guided imagery can help you focus your attention on pleasant scenarios that will help to relax your mind and body.[3] These exercises may help you feel less tension in your muscles and put your mind at ease.

You can practice visualization relaxation exercises as often as you wish. Visualization is a learned skill like any other healing tool in this book. The more you practice, the more skilled you will become at effectively using visualization.

Introduction for Visualization Exercises

This short script can be used at the beginning of each visualization exercise but is optional. The introduction will help your body prepare for the exercise by slowing down the breath and relaxing the nervous system.

---

2   Bala Kishore Batchu, "Neuro-Science Behind Visualization," International Coach Academy, December 3, 2013, https://coachcampus.com/coach-portfolios/research-papers/bala-kishore-batchu-neuro-science-behind-visualization/3.
3   National Center for Complementary and Integrative Health, "Relaxation Techniques for Health," May 10, 2018, https://nccih.nih.gov/health/stress/relaxation.htm.

Find a comfortable seated position and begin this visualization meditation by taking a deep breath in through your nose and out through your mouth.

Take a moment to focus your attention on your breathing without trying to change anything. Just notice your breathing, focusing intently on each breath.

(pause)

Let's practice slowing the rhythm of your breathing by counting.

Breathe in to the count of 4 . . .

(pause)

Hold for a count of 3 . . .

(pause)

Exhale to the count of 5 . . .

(pause)

Take a moment to relax your body. Get comfortable and notice how your body feels. If you need to make some slight adjustments to increase your comfort, give yourself permission to do that now. Take this time to close your eyes if you can and focus on your body sensations as you take another deep breath in . . . hold it . . . and breathe out, releasing tension.

Continue to breathe slowly . . . deeply.

As your body begins to relax and the stress starts to float away, roll your shoulders forward . . . and then roll your shoulders back. Repeat this once more . . . roll your shoulders forward . . . and then roll your shoulders back.

Take another deep breath.

Breathe in to the count of 4 . . .

(pause)

Hold for a count of 3 . . .

(pause)

Exhale to the count of 5 . . .

(pause)

As you visualize the following scene, let your body and mind become more and more relaxed with each moment. . . .

As you start to relax, create a picture in your mind. It is a warm summer day. Imagine that you are laying on a blanket outside. The blanket is soft, and the grass feels like a bed of clouds underneath your body. You look around and see trees beside you, a mix of leafy trees full of all different shades of green. Among the leaves you notice old tree trunks and watch as the branches move up and down as the wind blows them.

You look up and notice the bright blue sky above . . . as the clouds float by, the warm sun shines down and relaxes you, creating a calm, sleepy feeling.

The breeze feels cool and comfortable.

(pause)

You look at the clouds, you notice the different shapes. Some are round, fluffy clouds. Others are long, thin, wispy clouds. Some clouds look as though they were drawn with a paintbrush across the bright blue sky. The clouds drift by slowly . . . smoothly . . . silently.

As you sink into your cozy blanket on the soft grass, you begin to feel your body relaxing . . . bit by bit . . . feeling your muscles release . . . letting go of any tension . . . breathing in the healing air . . . breathing out any worries.

Take a deep breath in . . . and as you exhale, allow your body to relax. Continue to breathe slowly . . . deeply.

(pause)

You close your eyes again and listen to the calming sounds all around you. You hear the sounds of birds singing in the distance . . . the wind in the trees . . . the faint sounds of children playing and laughing. . . .

Imagine stillness in your body . . . and stillness in your mind. At this moment you are safe . . . at this moment you are at peace . . . there is nothing else to do but enjoy this moment gazing up at the sky, watching the clouds drift by, and enjoying this beautiful day.

Take another deep breath in through your nose and slowly exhale for 8 . . . 7 . . . 6 . . . 5 . . . 4 . . . 3 . . . 2 . . . 1 . . . allowing your body to completely relax.

When you are ready to leave this peaceful place, slowly begin to return your awareness to the present.

As you breathe, allow your body to reawaken. Bring yourself back to your usual level of awareness . . . wiggling your toes and fingers . . . feeling the energy flowing through your muscles.

While returning to a state of alertness, keep with you the feeling of calm and relaxation. When you are ready, open your eyes and return to your day feeling refreshed.

The Pond

[Begin here if *not* using the intro script]

Begin by taking a deep breath in and take a moment to relax your body. Get comfortable. Notice how your body feels. Take a deep breath in. Hold it . . . and breathe out, releasing tension. As you visualize the following scene, let your body and mind become more and more relaxed with each moment.

[Begin here if using the intro script]

Imagine yourself walking outdoors. It is not too warm and not too cold . . . it's a perfect spring day. You are walking among the trees . . . their leaves are moving in a slight breeze. You see a pond straight ahead glistening in the sun. You notice a wooden bench overlooking the private and serene woodland pond. As you walk toward the bench, you notice fish jumping up from the water, butterflies fluttering around the trees, and dragonflies flying back and forth as they soar over the water.

As you take a seat on the soft wooden bench, you close your

eyes and take a deep breath in . . . and exhale slowly . . . allowing your body to be completely relaxed.

Listening to all that surrounds you, you notice the frogs singing "ribbit" on their lily pads and busy bees buzzing around in the spring air. The birds begin chirping as you look up to the sky with your eyes closed and feel the warmth of the sun on your face . . . and there you are . . . totally still . . . utterly at rest. . . .

Continue to breathe slowly . . . deeply. Breathe in again, and as you exhale, allow your body to relax. Smell the grass . . . the wildflowers . . . the smell of the sun on the earth. . . .

As you open your eyes, you notice a small ladybug climbing up a blade of grass toward the top, pausing for a moment, and then flying away. You remember that ladybugs are good luck, and a small smile forms.

Look around again to see the sights around you. Notice how the pond water ripples as the fish swim back and forth. See the blue sky above you . . . the clouds slowly drifting by.

As you look out toward the lush green meadow, you notice a deer peeking out through the trees as it grazes at the flowers in the distance. The deer raises its head to look at you, sniffing the breeze, and then turns, disappearing silently among the trees.

Now it is time to leave the pond and return to the present. Wiggle your toes and fingers. Feel the surface beneath you. Listen for the sounds around you. Open your eyes to look around.

Take a moment to stretch your muscles and allow your body to reawaken. When you are ready, return to your usual activities, keeping with you a feeling of peace and calm.

The White Sandy Beach

[Begin here if *not* using the intro script]

Begin by relaxing your body. Relax your face by softening your eyes and release any tension in your forehead, your neck, and your throat. Soften your eyes and rest. Allow your breath to slow. Take a deep breath in . . . and a long breath out. . . .

[Begin here if using the intro script]

Allow your entire body to rest heavily on the surface where you are sitting. Now that your body is fully relaxed, let's take a trip to your favorite beach.

Imagine you are walking through a beautiful, tropical forest toward a white sandy beach. You feel safe, calm, and relaxed.

You hear the waves up ahead . . . you can smell the ocean . . . you can see the blue ocean water and hear the sounds of soft waves as the tide gently rolls in. The air is warm and flowing through your body . . . you feel a pleasant, cool breeze blowing through the trees.

As you come out of the forest into a long stretch of white sand . . . the beach is wide and long. . . . As you take off your shoes, you notice the sand feels like soft powder on your feet.

You can smell the clean salt air and see the incredible aqua color of the ocean ahead.

As you approach the water, you can feel the mist from the ocean on your skin. You walk closer to the waves and feel the sand becoming wet and firm. . . .

A wave crashes and the water comes quickly to shore . . . as you step forward, you feel the cool temperature of the water provide relief from the warm sand on your toes before the water returns into the abyss of the ocean.

As you walk farther into the clear blue water, allow the visualization relaxation to deepen. . . .

Just enjoy the ocean for a few minutes . . . notice the pleasant, relaxing temperature . . . becoming more and more relaxing . . . providing relief from the hot sun . . . cool, but not cold. . . .

As you begin to walk along the edge of the water . . . you are free of worries, free of stress, and full of peace. . . .

When you are ready, walk out of the water toward a comfortable lounge chair and towel, just for you. Feel the weight of your body sinking into your beach chair, the warmth of the sand on your feet, and the large umbrella keeping you slightly shaded, creating just the right temperature.

The only thing to do right at this moment is to just be still and enjoy the sun on your face, the breeze in your hair, and the waves on your toes. . . .

Allow all of your stress to melt away . . . feeling calm . . . feeling at peace . . . feeling refreshed. . . .

When you are ready to leave the beach, do so very slowly. . . .

As you bring yourself back to your usual level of alertness and awareness, begin to open your eyes, wiggle your toes and fingers, and feel the surface beneath you. Listen for the sounds around you, and as you become fully alert . . . you feel refreshed and energized . . . and calm and relaxed. . . .

Take a moment to stretch your muscles and allow your body to reawaken. When you are ready, return to your usual activities, keeping with you feelings of peace and calm.

The Safe Place

[Begin here if *not* using the intro script]

Begin by finding a comfortable position. For the next few moments, focus on calming your mind by paying attention to your breath. Allow your breath to center and relax you. Relax your face by softening your eyes and release any tension in your forehead, your neck, and your throat. Soften your eyes and rest.

As your breath begins to slow, focus on your belly and feel it rise up on the inhale and fall down on the exhale. . . .

Take a deep breath in through your nose . . .

(pause)

and a long breath out through your mouth. . . .

[Begin here if using the intro script]

As you begin this visualization, remember that you are safe at this moment. You will be guided to imagine a setting or scenic environment where you feel totally comfortable and at peace.

This will be a place you can return to any time you feel you need to find solace from a busy and hectic world . . . this visualization will help to relax your mind and guide you to imagine your own peaceful, safe place.

Now begin to create a picture in your mind of a place where you can completely relax. Where is this peaceful place? Maybe it is somewhere outdoors . . . or indoors . . . maybe it is a place where you have been before or somewhere that you long to go. . . .

(pause)

Now picture some more details about your safe place. . . . What does this place look like? Is your safe place small? Big?

What colors . . . shapes . . . objects . . . do you see? Is there water? Are there plants? Animals? Birds? What are the beautiful things that make your place enjoyable?

Who is with you? Or maybe you are alone? Imagine who is at your place, whether it is just you or if you have company . . . and notice that you feel completely safe. . . .

Focus now on the relaxing sounds around you in your peaceful place. . . . What sounds do you hear around you? Or perhaps it is silent? Pay attention to the sounds that are more noticeable and those that are more subtle. Are these sounds far away or close by?

Drifting away into this safe place, you feel more and more relaxed . . . more and more at peace. . . .

Next focus on any skin sensations. . . . What do you notice about the sensations of touch? Do you notice the earth beneath you? Or whatever you are sitting or lying on? What is the temperature like? Notice any breeze that may be present . . . all creating your safe place full of relaxation and stillness. . . .

Think about any tastes or smells you may notice about your place. . . .

Maybe you give your peaceful and safe place a name . . . it might be just one word or a phrase that you can use to bring that image back any time you need to.

Now that you have a picture of this safe place, imagine yourself there. What are you doing in this calming place? Maybe you are just sitting and enjoying the peaceful feeling of this moment . . . maybe you are walking around or doing any variety of activities. . . .

Picture yourself in this place completely at peace, becoming more aware of your breath as you slowly breathe in . . .

(pause)

and slowly breathe out. . . .

This is a safe place . . . a place of calm . . . a place of peace . . . a place where you have no worries, cares, or concerns . . . a place where you can simply enjoy just being . . . no pressures . . . no deadlines . . . no pain . . . no fears . . . just love and safety.

You can rest in your safe place for a while and just enjoy the peacefulness and serenity. . . .

When you are ready to leave your safe place, slowly begin to turn your attention back to the present moment. . . .

As you bring yourself back to your usual level of alertness and awareness, begin to open your eyes, wiggle your toes and fingers, and feel the surface beneath you. Listen for the sounds around you, and as you become fully alert . . . you feel refreshed and energized . . . calm and relaxed. . . .

Take a moment to stretch your muscles and allow your body to reawaken. When you are ready, return to your usual activities and file away the imaginary place in your mind . . . it will always be there for you the next time you need it. As you return to your everyday life, remember to keep with you the feeling of calm from your peaceful place.

If you are reading the visualizations to yourself, it is recommended to put on some relaxing music (instrumental/meditative is best) and find someplace quiet with no distractions. After reading through the scripts, close your eyes and imagine yourself in that relaxing place. If you are listening to the scripts, get a pair of headphones, sit somewhere away from distractions, and get your favorite blanket or cozy pajamas on and drift away.

HAPPY MEMORY VISUALIZATION

Find a comfortable and quiet place. Close your eyes and create a blank canvas in your mind. Think back to a memory where you felt utterly happy and carefree. Visualize every detail of that memory.

If you don't remember a specific detail, fill it in with whatever comes to mind. Where were you? What were you wearing? Who were you with? What was the environment like?

Picture the room or location of the memory and everything about it. What do you see? Hear? Touch? Smell? Taste?

As you notice more and more detail, you become more and more relaxed.

Once the image is complete in your mind, spend a few minutes there just enjoying the memory.

When you are ready, come back to right now and face the rest of your day with a fresh mind.

Bonus Healing Activity
My Happy Memory Exercise

Write about a happy memory below. Picture the room or location of the memory and describe everything about it. What were you wearing? Who were you with? What was the environment like? What emotions are you experiencing? What did you see? Hear? Feel? Smell? Taste?

My Happy Memory

_____

_____

_____

_____

_____

_____

_____

_____

_____

_____

DOUBLE-PANED WINDOW TECHNIQUE

So your mind is racing . . . whether you're overloaded at work or worried about the future, sometimes those unwanted thoughts take over. The double-paned window visualization can be useful if you're looking to quiet a spiraling, anxious brain.

1. Picture a bunch of people chatting loudly outside your open window.
2. Instead of yelling at them, since you have a double-paned window, you just calmly close it.
3. Imagine that the chatting is silenced when the window is fully closed, and you can drift off to sleep without background conversations.

CREATIVE VISUALIZATION

A creative visualization is a mindfulness exercise that can be helpful in the midst of a stressful situation and can be used to promote success in every area of life. Shakti Gawain, a pioneer in the field of personal development and internationally renowned teacher of consciousness, describes creative visualization as "the technique of using your imagination to create what you want in your life."[4] Gawain suggests that everything is energy, including thoughts. Certain thoughts and feelings attract similar types of energy; therefore we attract into our lives what

---

4   Shakti Gawain, _Creative Visualization: Use the Power of Your Imagination to Create What You Want in Your Life_ (Novato, CA: Nataraj Publishing, 2002).

we think about the most, believe in strongest, and imagine most vividly. Gawain goes on to say,

> When we are negative and fearful, insecure or anxious, we often attract the very experiences, situations, or people that we are seeking to avoid. If we are positive in attitude, expecting and envisioning pleasure, satisfaction, and happiness, we tend to attract and create people, situations, and events that conform to our positive expectations.
>
> This means that consciously imagining what we want in life can help us to manifest it in reality. By using creative visualization, you create a clear image of the goals you want to manifest (emotional, mental, physical, and spiritual). If you begin to visualize the life you want, you may begin to experience the emotions connected to this image—as if it were true.
>
> You may start to feel motivated to create new goals for yourself. Creative visualization can help you to achieve these goals and manifest the outcomes you desire. By applying creative visualization consistently and focusing on these images with positive energy, your dreams may become a reality!

Four Steps of Creative Visualization

Step 1: Choose a Goal

Think of something you want to have or to happen. Decide on something you would like to have, work toward, or create. Some examples are a job, a relationship, a house, a happier state of mind, improved health, a better physical condition, or a change in yourself. It really can be anything that you would like to achieve!

Step 2: Create a Clear Mental Picture of the Outcome You Want

Create a picture in your mind of the object or situation exactly as you want it. Make this image vivid, with lots of details. Think of it in the present tense as already existing the way you want it to be. It's almost as if you are

Creative Visualization Exercise

Step 1
Write about something you would like to have, work toward, or create.

Step 2
How do you picture your life when you achieve this?

Step 3
How can you make sure that you visualize this throughout your day?

Step 4
Write some strong positive statements to yourself about this goal.

already living it. How do you desire it to be right now? Make yourself part of the picture and see yourself enjoying the object or situation.

Step 3: Focus on This Image Throughout Your Day

Focus on the image you created in Step 2 on a consistent basis every day. Picture it often throughout your day, during regular activities and in meditative periods. Without pressuring yourself to make something happen, just bring that image along with you as you go through your day.

Step 4: Give the Image Positive Energy

As you focus on your goal, imagine that the best possible outcome is happening right now. Think of this image in a positive, encouraging way. Make strong positive statements to yourself about this goal. See yourself receiving or achieving it using positive affirmations (review the following affirmation list or review chapter 5 for examples). During this stage, try to temporarily suspend any doubts or disbelief you may have, at least for the moment. Practice believing that what you desire is very real and possible.

Bonus Healing Activity

Create a Vision Board

A vision board, or a dream board, is a board or display filled with images, pictures, and affirmations of your goals, dreams, and desires. A vision board is designed to serve as a source of inspiration and motivation. It is filled with images of how you want to feel, what you want to do, what you want to have, and who you want to be. Many people believe that they can attract into their life what they envision. A vision board can be used to manifest your ideal life on paper.

How to Create a Vision Board

Supplies:

- Blank paper/poster board (if you don't have poster paper you can use a notebook, journal, box, or envelope)

- Scissors
- Glue
- Markers
- Crayons or colored pencils
- Pen and pencil
- Magazines
- Newspaper
- Catalogs
- Quotes, affirmation, phrases
- Images of choice from internet
- Photos
- Drawings

Instructions:

1. Go through your supplies and choose images, photos, and words that resonate with you and your goals/dreams.
2. Cut out desired photos, images, and words.
3. Glue your chosen photos, images, and words on the paper/poster board.
4. Hang your vision board in a place where you will see it often. Since the board displays all that you want to focus on in your life, it is helpful to hang it up somewhere you can see and focus on every day.

The more you look at your vision board, the more you will visualize your goals and dreams! The more you see and visualize, the more you will stay focused on achieving those goals and dreams. You are bringing energy to those goals to make them a reality.

Digital Vision Boards

If you don't want to gather all the materials for a physical vision board, you can also use digital technology to create your dream! Here are some tips on how to use technology to create your vision board.

- Use online platforms such as Pinterest or Canva to create the collage.
- Put the images or collage on your phone to remind you of your goals.
- Print out your digital vision board and put it on your wall, mirror, or refrigerator.

Short Creative Visualization for Stress

Practice this visualization any time you begin to ruminate about a problem that you need to be resolved. Record this script in your own voice or ask a safe person in your support group to record this script in their voice. When you begin to feel out of control because of a stressful situation, listen to or read this script to imagine the problem as resolved. This may help you to more clearly and logically come up with a solution to your problem.

Sit comfortably in a peaceful place . . . close your eyes and take a deep breath in through your nose . . . and a slow breath out through your mouth.

Clear your mind and think of only this moment right now . . . no stress . . . no worries . . . only peace. . . .

Begin to picture yourself on the other side of whatever stressful situation may be going on for you right now.

Imagine that this situation has been completely resolved . . . it's not important how it was resolved . . . it's not important to focus on solutions . . . simply just visualize what life will be like once the situation resolves itself.

Take another deep breath in for 4 . . . and breathe out for 6. . . .

Using your senses, picture every detail about this situation as it is resolved. What are you wearing? What do you see around you? What colors do you notice? What are you saying? Who are you saying it to? What type of room are you in? What is in your environment? What type of objects in your visualized environment can you touch or feel? What do they feel like?

Take a deep breath in for 4 . . . and breathe out for 6. . . .

You may now be able to see a solution to your situation. If you can't, that's okay, too. This visualization is meant for you to recognize that all feelings are temporary and in time you will feel in control again.

When you are visualizing what it will be like to have the problem resolved, the solution may come to you in the midst of your visualization. This may lower or eliminate your stress about the situation.

Now open your eyes . . . and remind yourself that you are in control . . . this will be resolved. . . .

FUTURE SELF-VISUALIZATION

Visualizing your future in a hopeful and positive way can help rewire your brain to believe that you are capable of healing. These writing prompts will help you to think about your healing progress in a promising way and help you to create a new story for your future self.

Goals

Be as specific as possible. Imagine the outcome of achieving that goal. Be as descriptive as possible. Focus on the senses you might experience during that time. How would you feel? What would you smell? What would you see?

My short-term goals are:

_____

_____

_____

My long-term goals are:

_____

_____

_____

Your Future Self Writing Exercise

Imagine you are meeting your future self for the first time. Picture how you envision your best self in the future. Be as concrete and descriptive as possible. You can use this tool to visualize your future self and keep yourself accountable to becoming this person.

Use These Questions as a Guide

- What does this person, the future you, look like? What are you wearing?
- Where does your "future self" live? What are the colors of the place? Is anyone else there?
- What are you doing with your life now? What do you love about your life?
- What do I need to know to get me from where I am now to where you are? What would be most helpful? Listen to what your future self has to tell you.
- Think of any current anxieties or stressors. Let your future self know that you are feeling worried, scared, and hurt. Ask your future self, "How did you overcome this challenge or heartache?"
- Finally, ask your future self to tell you one word that is important for you to remember when you're feeling down or need support to keep going toward your goals. What is that one word? Remember it.

My Future Self

_____

_____

_____

_____

_____

VISUALIZATION EXERCISES TO ADD
TO MY HEALING TOOL KIT

_____

_____

_____

_____

_____

CHAPTER 7

Distraction Ideas to Use Anywhere

A distraction technique is simply any activity that you engage in to redirect your mind off your current emotions. Instead of putting all your energy into the upsetting emotion, refocus your attention on something else. When you distract yourself, you can manage your strong emotions by bringing your focus elsewhere. Although distraction is not a long-term solution, using a distraction technique in times of high anxiety can provide an initial sense of relief and control, helping to reduce the intensity of anxiety indicators. Distraction is an effective way of putting your mind on something other than the symptoms you are experiencing simply because it is difficult for the mind to focus on more than one thing at the same time. This chapter includes brain games, movement strategies, and writing prompts that will help distract your anxious brain when you begin to start feeling out of control.

HEALING IN ACTION
CHANGE YOUR ENVIRONMENT

It can be very helpful to leave where you are and move your body. If you are sitting on your couch at home, get up for some fresh air. If you can, make sure to get some movement flowing in your body. Some activities include taking a walk outside, going for a drive, doing a yoga video, or getting lunch at your favorite restaurant.

What are some ways you can change your environment or move your body when you are feeling anxious?

Sing the Anxiety Away

Sing or hum the worry away! Singing or humming helps the fear center of the brain to calm itself. Think of a song that you can hum to whenever you're feeling overwhelmed. If you can't think of a song at the moment, take a deep breath in through your nose and hum the breath out.

What are three songs that make you happy?

1. _____
2. _____
3. _____

Listen to Music and DANCE!

By listening very intently to a song, it is almost impossible for your worries to overpower the music. Moving your body and dancing to an upbeat song will help to distract you from your intrusive thoughts and help calm the fear center of your brain.

List three of your favorite dance songs:

1. _____
2. _____
3. _____

Best Distraction Apps

Some of the apps that I recommend for my patients include:
- 1010!
- Tetris
- Word Search Pro

- Wordscapes
- 2048
- Jigsaw Planet
- Geoguessr
- Dots
- Angry Birds
- Six!
- Nonogram
- Pixel Art
- Elevate
- Candy Crush
- Animal Restaurant
- SimCity
- Homescapes
- Lily's Garden

Which apps help you the most? List them here:

_____

_____

_____

_____

_____

Entertain Yourself

Read something that interests you (e.g., book, magazine, cookbook, newspaper). If reading isn't your thing, you may want to try watching TV or a movie to set your mind on something else. Research has also shown that playing video games can be effective for distracting people from anxiety.

Ways to entertain yourself:
- Listen to soothing music.
- Cuddle with pets.
- Eat your favorite snack or have a cup of tea.
- Take a long walk.
- Exercise.

- Do yoga.
- Play a sport.
- Read a book or magazine.
- Knit.
- Complete a puzzle.
- Color.
- Paint.
- Craft.
- Build models.
- Play a video game (calming ones, not adrenaline-inducing games).

In what ways can you entertain yourself when anxious?

_____

_____

_____

_____

_____

CONNECT TO YOUR SUPPORT SYSTEM

Another way to help distract yourself when feeling anxious is by reaching out to a friend or loved one. Can you think of at least three people you could reach out to right now? Think of the people in your life with whom you feel emotionally safe. Feeling "safe" with another person means that you feel comfortable with being authentic around that person and sharing your thoughts, feelings, and ideas with them. Feeling safe with another person means that you can freely and openly express yourself without the fear of being judged, criticized, ignored, or silenced.

When you reach out to your "safe" person, remember to be open and honest about your thoughts and feelings, but be careful not to spend all your time talking about negative emotions. Research shows that ruminating over negative emotions can create more anxiety. When used in this sense, ruminating is defined as "repetitively going over a thought or a problem without completion."[1] If you struggle with depression or anxiety, this type of intrusive thinking can often include feelings of worthlessness and failure. These feelings of inadequacy then can increase anxiety, which then interferes with solving the problem . . . and cue a deeper depression.

So try to find a balance when reaching out for support. Remember, your "safe" person should not be a person that you *have to* depend on to self-soothe (this would be considered a codependent relationship, which can hurt the healing process). Your support system should help comfort you and show you compassion, but not be your only way to heal.

On-the-Go Activity

1. Think of at least three "safe" people in your life.
2. Who can you text or call if you start to feel anxious?
3. What type of support do you need when you're anxious? (Knowing more about your needs can help your "safe" person effectively support you.)

DISTRACT YOURSELF BY WRITING IT OUT

Writing exercises can be another powerful tool for distraction. One of the most healing writing exercises is journaling. Journaling is a wonderful way to tap into your emotional self while gaining insights into your intrusive thinking patterns. Through this type of writing process, you can refocus and adjust to managing your emotions.

Pick a few of the following prompts to help shift your anxious mind-set:

- What would it feel like if you completely let go of a situation?
- The most peaceful place I have ever visited or heard about is . . .
- Aside from intrusive thoughts, some other things that keep me up at night are . . . What would it be like if I eliminated them from my life for thirty days?
- Here is what I would tell my best friend if they were struggling and called me right now.

1   J. M. Smith and L. B. Alloy, "A Roadmap to Rumination: A Review of the Definition, Assessment, and Conceptualization of this Multifaceted Construct," *Clinical Psychology Review* 29, no. 2 (March 2009): 116–28, doi:10.1016/j.cpr.2008.10.003.

- The funniest movie I ever watched was . . . This movie made me laugh so hard because . . .
- My favorite accomplishment is . . .
- Ten things I love about myself are . . .
- One thing I wish I could change is . . .
- I felt really happy when . . .
- Five things I am grateful for today are . . .
- If a friend was feeling anxious, what would I say to the friend to help them feel better?
- If I am feeling stressed, I know that following five things will make me feel better (add at least one of these things to your to-do list) . . .
- A time when I couldn't stop laughing was . . . and I was with . . . I felt . . .
- Create a list of things you want to accomplish this month or year.
- Five things that made me smile today were . . .
- These are three people who support me and make me feel safe . . . They make me feel emotionally safe because . . .
- List three reasons why I matter . . .

DISTRACTION HEALING GAMES

These distraction healing games are a great way to redirect your thoughts any time, anywhere. If you feel more overwhelmed in the car, at a party, on an airplane, or in a grocery store, these types of distraction strategies will help keep you present and grounded rather than anxious and panicked.

- Say the alphabet backward.
- Name all the ice cream flavors that you can think of.
- Name all your favorite musicians.
- Think of names beginning with the letters T, A, C, or M.
- Name all the candy brand names that come to mind.

- Name as many cities around the world as you can.
- Count by 7s as high as you can (or any other odd interval).
- Play the "guess their occupation" game. Look at people around you and try to guess their jobs or occupations, or where they are going.
- Look up today's date. Repeat to yourself the day of the week, month, year, time of day, and where you are currently. Remind yourself that you are in this moment, not in the past, and right now you are safe.
- Notice the season it is outside, what the sky looks like. Name the street you are on and the zip code.
- Play the categories game with yourself. Choose a category such as colors, animals, or foods, and try to name at least ten things in that category. You can also use the alphabet and try to name something in that category for each letter of the alphabet, beginning with A, B, C, and so on.
- Choose a shape (triangle, oval, square) and try to find all of the objects around you of that shape. You can also do this with colors—for example, find all of the green things in the room.

THE "BEST OF" TECHNIQUE

Make a "best of" list. You can do this exercise using a pad of paper or just keeping a mental list. Use these questions to distract yourself when you begin to feel overwhelmed.

- Top ten favorite books?
- Favorite actors of all time?
- What are the ten most memorable music videos of the decade?
- Top five favorite podcasts?
- Top five documentaries that have made the most impact on your life?

- If you could have dinner with anyone, which four people would you invite to the table?

WALK OUT THE DISTRACTIONS

If you are able to move your body when feeling anxious, then do it. If you can go outside right now, do it. Even a five-minute walk around the block can help to ground you in a way that can bring you back to reality. While on your walk, start to notice and describe all the things around you that you can see. Some things may be mundane, but you will start to notice little things that would have completely passed you by; maybe a pretty pink flower growing (bonus points if you smell the flower), a baby giggling, a leaf blowing in the wind, or a bright red door on the home you're walking past.

On-the-Go Activity

Take a small notepad with you, write down five things you can see, and describe these things in detail, noting their color, shape, etc. Write down four things you can hear, three things you can touch, and two things you can smell.

THE CATEGORIES GAME

Find one thing in each category starting with each letter of the alphabet:
- Books
- Movies
- Cities
- Countries
- Fruits
- Songs
- Actors
- Disney films
- Things you would find in a classroom

Name as Many as You Can

- Presidents
- Breakfast foods
- Sodas
- Restaurant chains
- Condiments
- US capitals
- Kitchen appliances
- Furniture in the house
- Cartoons
- Eighties songs
- Musical artists

CREATE A LIST OF "HAPPIES"

This is a great way to retrain your brain to a more positive train of thinking. Create a list of happy things you have seen or experienced today. They can be life-changing events such as getting married or landing the dream job, or they can be smaller things such as taking a walk in nature or seeing a beautiful sunny sky. Complete this "happy list" any time you begin to feel overwhelmed, stressed, or anxious.

Happy Prompts

- A time when someone was kind to you
- A compliment someone gave you in the previous week
- A place where you felt calm
- A moment when you felt loved
- The last thing that made you belly-laugh
- An object that makes you smile

Write your list of "happies" here:

_____

_____

_____

_____

_____

DISTRACTION IDEAS TO ADD
TO MY HEALING TOOL KIT

_____

_____

_____

_____

_____

Part III

CREATE YOUR HEALING TOOL KIT

CHAPTER 8

Self-Advocacy:
The Unspoken Healer

L et's face it, the healing tools in this book are wonderful coping techniques, but making lifelong changes means looking deeper into the underlying reason or reasons for your anxiety. There are a number of factors that may contribute to poor mental health and a number of reasons why someone may struggle with anxiety daily. Factors that influence mental health include genetics, family upbringing, social support, education, environment, and access to resources. While some of these factors may be out of our hands, we can control the choices we make when it comes to healing. This includes the choice to be our own best wellness advocate.

Without being able to advocate for yourself and ask specific questions, you may not always get the treatment that is best for you. While this guide is a great start to educating yourself on anxiety and what you can do to help heal it, part of that process may be finding the right health care professional to help support and guide you through the healing journey.

THE PRIMARY-CARE DOCTOR'S VISIT

So how do you find the right professional to help heal? Well, that takes time, research, and some trial and error. Many people will initially go to their primary-care doctor when experiencing symptoms of anxiety or depression, in the hope of getting some guidance. During these appointments you may feel stuck, lost, or confused. You may feel like the doctor is rushing you, leaving you even more discouraged than when you first got there. Sure, the doctor will check your body to make sure nothing is wrong physically, but how about what is happening psychologically? This is why it is important that you get all of the information you need to make an educated decision on your treatment. This takes self-advocacy. Following are some questions that can help you advocate for you and your anxiety at your next primary-care doctor's visit.

Healing tip: Make a copy of this page and bring to your appointment.

Questions to Ask a Doctor or Psychiatrist:

1. What are my treatment options for anxiety?
2. Are there any underlying medical problems that could be causing my anxiety symptoms?
3. Do you recommend medication? If so, will I take it every day, or as needed? How long will I need to take it?
4. What side effects can I expect from these medications? Is there a way to minimize or prevent side effects? What should I do if I miss a dose of medication?
5. Would therapy be helpful? If so, which type and for how long?
6. How long before I can expect to feel better?
7. Once treated, how likely is it that my anxiety symptoms will return?
8. What lifestyle changes can I make to help me feel better?
9. How will alcohol or other drugs interact with my medication or affect my anxiety?
10. Are there holistic ways to treat my anxiety? If so, what are they?
11. What does functional medicine mean? What does integrative medicine mean?

When it comes to anxiety, diet and eating patterns play a major role in our mood and mental health. But what many people fail to recognize is that food is medicine. Basically, what you choose to put into your body will influence how you feel both physically and mentally. If you prioritize consuming enough healthy foods and eating regularly throughout the day, you may be amazed by the difference proper nutrition can make for your health and well-being.

Make sure to talk with a doctor before making any considerable changes in your diet. It may be helpful to involve a functional medicine doctor, dietitian, or nutritionist (your doctor can refer you to one or you may want to do your own research). An integrated treatment approach may include talk therapy, mindfulness techniques, emotional regulation tools, good sleep hygiene, and a balanced diet. All are equally important parts of your care.

Healing tip: Make a copy of this page and bring to your appointment.

Questions to Ask a Functional Doctor/Nutritionist/Dietitian:

1. Is what I eat linked to anxiety and depression?
2. What is the brain/gut connection?
3. Are there certain foods that create anxiety?
4. Does anti-inflammatory food help decrease anxiety?
5. What holistic supplements are known to help reduce anxiety?
6. Are there vitamins that help balance moods?
7. What are omega-3 fats?
8. I have been diagnosed with irritable bowel syndrome (IBS). Is that linked to anxiety or depression? If it is, how so?
9. Do caffeine and alcohol affect anxiety? If yes, how so?
10. Is the intake of sugar connected to anxiety and depression? If yes, how so?

This guide is all about helping you create a holistic and integrative anxiety tool kit to help you heal—for good. One of those tools may include a therapist. My therapist is one of the most essential "tools" in my tool kit. She is an incredible support person who has helped me through some of the darkest times, and I value her guidance. A question I get in my Instagram DMs daily is "How do I find the right therapist?" Well, I wish it was that simple. Finding a therapist that you truly connect with can take a lot of time, money, and self-advocacy. The truth is, finding the right therapist is like dating. You may have to go through several different therapists before finally finding "the one." I know that may sound tedious, but by asking the right questions, you can help streamline the search. Following are some suggested questions that may help during the initial phone call with a potential therapist.

Healing tip: Make a copy of this page and bring to your appointment.

Questions to Ask a Therapist:

1. What type of therapy do you specialize in?
2. Do you have any areas of expertise?
3. Will you collaborate with my other health care providers if I give permission?
4. What are the differences among a psychotherapist, psychologist, psychiatrist, and social worker?
5. Do you give homework? What does that look like?
6. How often will I come to session?
7. What is your view on medication?
8. How long are sessions?
9. How important is the therapeutic relationship to you?
10. What does your confidentiality statement look like?
11. What is your therapy approach?
12. How long will treatment last?

COMPARING THE COUNSELING PROFESSIONALS

Many times, knowing where to start when looking for a "therapist" or "counselor" can not only be tedious but also confusing! If you don't work in the health care field, it's likely that you may not know the differences among a psychologist, psychotherapist, psychiatrist, and social worker. The truth is, there really isn't any education regarding the terminology of mental health professionals, unless you seek the information on your own. If you are currently looking for a mental health professional, then make sure to read the following information closely. I have provided a short "cheat sheet" on the different types of mental health professionals that will hopefully give you a better understanding of the type of clinician that may best suit your needs.

PSYCHOTHERAPIST

This is an umbrella term for any mental health professional who is trained to treat people for their emotional problems. Psychotherapists have special training in psychology and counseling and complete graduate school to get their masters or doctoral degree to become practicing therapists. Psychotherapists may be licensed and specialize in helping clients develop better cognitive skills and cope with various life challenges to improve their lives. Depending upon their academic degree, a psychotherapist can be a psychiatrist, psychologist, or social worker and work with individuals, couples, groups, or families.

Credentials:

- MA (master of arts)
- MS (master of science)
- LPC (licensed professional counselor)
- LMHC (licensed mental health counselor)
- LCPC (licensed clinical professional counselor)
- LPCC (licensed professional clinical counselor of mental health)
- LCMHC (licensed clinical mental health counselor)
- LMHP (licensed mental health practitioner)

PSYCHOLOGIST

A psychologist usually has a PhD and provides talk therapy along with training in psychological testing. Psychologists who concentrate on research generally work in academic or research settings. There are some psychologists who are trained specifically to do clinical work (rather than research) and graduate with a PsyD (doctorate of psychology) rather than a PhD. They can also perform research assessments as well as focus on providing psychotherapy (talk therapy) to help clients.

Credentials:
- PhD (doctor of philosophy)
- PsyD (doctor of psychology)
- EdD (doctor of education)

PSYCHIATRIST (PSYCHOPHARMACOLOGIST)

A psychiatrist has a medical degree and is often referred to as a psychopharmacologist. They become a medical doctor before doing specialist training in mental health and have a stronger sense of biology and neurochemistry in the brain. Because they are medical doctors, psychiatrists understand the links between mental and physical problems. The main duty of a psychiatrist is to provide prescriptions and medication management. Some psychiatrists continue to practice psychotherapy, but it is rare. Most intake appointments are approximately forty-five minutes to an hour and follow-up appointments are about fifteen minutes, although this varies on a case-by-case basis. It is recommended that you see a psychotherapist additionally for talk therapy if you are not receiving treatment from a psychiatrist.

Credentials:
- MD (doctor of medicine)
- DO (doctor of osteopathic medicine)

SOCIAL WORKER

Social workers have a master's degree and are most widely known to provide social services in hospitals and agencies. Some other social workers also practice psychotherapy but do not provide psychological testing.

Credentials:

- MSW (master of social work)
- LCSW (licensed clinical social worker)
- LSW (licensed social worker)
- LCSW-C (licensed certified social worker-clinical)
- LGSW (licensed graduate social worker)
- LICSW (licensed independent clinical social worker)
- LISW (licensed independent social worker)
- LMSW (licensed master social worker)

YOUR SAFETY SUPPORT SYSTEM

When creating your healing tool kit, keep in mind the people around you who help you feel supported and safe when you are anxious. This may be family members, friends, or professional colleagues. This is all part of the healing journey. Research has shown that having a strong support system can reduce stress and that a safe support system has many positive benefits, including higher levels of well-being, better coping skills, and a longer and healthier life.[1] If you have a select number of people in your life that you can trust and turn to in times of need, it is more likely that you will be able to manage everyday challenges, make difficult decisions, and handle a crisis situation. The level of support that you receive from these individuals may vary, but these people are able to provide you with the emotional support you need when you feel out of control or anxious.

It can be hard to know how to find your true support system, and it may even include people you haven't even met yet; but keep speaking your truth and you will find your safe people. There are others out there who know exactly what you are going through and want to take your pain away. Always keep speaking your truth and remember that you are worthy and loved no matter what. Learning to regulate your body and mind on your

1   T. F. Harandi, M. M. Taghinasab, and T. D. Nayeri, "The Correlation of Social Support with Mental Health: A Meta-Analysis," *Electronic Physician* 9, no. 9 (September 2017): 5212–22, doi:10.19082/5212.

own is the pathway to healing, but human connection will always be a vital part of this process.

HEALING IN ACTION: SELF-REFLECTION

Answer these questions to learn how you can best advocate for yourself.

How can I best advocate for my physical health?

_____

_____

What action steps can I take to advocate for my mental health?

_____

_____

Who are three people that make me feel safe?

_____

_____

Why do these individuals make me feel safe?

_____

_____

SUPPORT SYSTEM TO ADD TO MY HEALING TOOL KIT

_____

_____

_____

_____

_____

CHAPTER 9

Create Your
Anxiety-Healing Tool Kit

T ime to start focusing on *you*! This chapter includes specific activities to help you find what unique tools from this guide work best for you when anxious. Create your own healing tool kit based on the strategies you have practiced and use this chapter for reference whenever you begin to feel anxiety coming on.

WHAT WORKS FOR YOU?
DOING THE THINGS THAT HELP

The goal of this guide is to help you create the healing tool kit that works specifically for you. This may take some trial and error, but once you have recognized what tools truly work to help calm your mind and body, you are on the right path toward healing!

Start creating your healing tool kit by paying special attention to what you were doing when the panic attacks ended. What was the action step you took to help to activate your relaxation response? Is there a specific behavior that seemed to correlate with the time the panic attacks subsided? For example, if you notice that your panic attacks subsided at about the same time you went through the five-senses exercise, or when you splashed cold water on your face, or when you practiced EFT tapping, then those techniques should all be included in your healing tool kit!

To help you start building your own anxiety-healing tool kit, I've shared mine as an example here:

ALISON'S ANXIETY-HEALING TOOL KIT

Self-Soothing Items

- Heating pad
- Eye mask
- Fidget spinner
- Silly Putty
- Weighted blanket
- My dog
- My journal
- Working out while watching reality TV
- Walking on the beach
- Listening to podcasts
- Sitting in a hot tub

Breathing Techniques

- Belly breathing
- Four-square breathing
- Alternate nostril breathing

Support System

- My sister, Amy
- My parents
- My "safe" friends Dorothy, Jenny, Rita, and Kelley
- My therapist

Coping Statements

- I am safe.
- I have felt like this before and have gotten through it.
- This feeling is only temporary.
- I take one step at a time.
- It is okay just to rest right now. There is nowhere I have to be.
- This will be over soon.
- Don't think; just breathe.
- Your thoughts do not have control.

Meditations

- Insight Timer playlists
- Walking meditation

Visualization Exercises

- My Happy Place
- The Serene Beach Scene
- Private Garden

Supplements

- Vitamin D
- Vitamin B$_{12}$
- CBD oil
- Ginger tea
- Collagen
- Magnesium

Apps

- Insight Timer
- Calm
- Progressive Muscle Relaxation
- 1010!

Videos

- EFT tapping clips
- Yoga for anxiety videos
- *The Office* scenes

Books

- *The Feeling Good Handbook* by David Burns
- *Love Yourself, Heal Your Life Workbook* by Louise Hay
- *The Anxiety and Worry Workbook* by Aaron T. Beck and David A. Clark
- *How to Do the Work* by Dr. Nicole LePera

Podcasts and Audiobooks

- *The Power of Vulnerability* by Brene Brown
- *Unlocking Us*, with Brene Brown
- *Super Soul Conversations*, with Oprah Winfrey
- *Mark Groves Podcast*
- *The Daily Meditation Podcast* by Mary Meckley
- *Meditation Minis Podcast* by Chel Hamilton
- *On Purpose*, with Jay Shetty

Distraction Ideas

- TV shows: *The Office, Schitt's Creek, Girls*
- Movie: *Bridesmaids*
- Journal prompts
- 1010! app

Sleep Hygiene

- Noise machine
- Going to bed and waking up at the same time every day
- Eye mask
- Sleep stories (from the Insight Timer app)
- Diffuser in room with calming essential oils
- Lavender spray on pillow
- Avoiding coffee
- Avoiding alcohol

Grounding Tools and Exercises

- Ten-minute walk outside
- Breathing fresh air
- Putting my bare feet on the grass
- Splashing cold water on my face
- Sucking on ice
- Yoga
- EFT tapping
- Painting with my niece and nephew
- Listening to soft music
- Organizing my room/belongings (e.g., putting away laundry, decluttering things)
- Acupuncture

Two-Minute Relief Tools

- Two-minute senses grounding tool
- Mindful music exercise
- Music to match your mood exercise
- Body scan
- PMR

YOUR ANXIETY-HEALING TOOL KIT

Self-Soothing Items

_____
_____
_____
_____

Breathing Techniques

_____
_____
_____
_____

Support System

_____
_____
_____
_____

Coping Statements

_____

_____

_____

_____

Meditations

_____

_____

_____

_____

Visualization Exercises

_____

_____

_____

_____

Supplements

_____

_____

_____

_____

Apps

_____

_____

_____

_____

Videos

_____

_____

_____

_____

Books

_____

_____

_____

_____

Podcasts and Audiobooks

_____

_____

_____

_____

Distraction Ideas

_____

_____

_____

_____

Sleep Hygiene

_____

_____

_____

_____

Grounding Tools and Exercises

_____

_____

_____

_____

Two-Minute Relief Tools

_____

_____

_____

_____

CHAPTER 10

The Anxiety-Healing Workbook

This bonus chapter is all about taking action and changing behavior when your mind begins racing. This chapter includes anxiety-healing workbook activities and worksheets complete with coloring pages, distraction games, cognitive reframing worksheets, anxiety-coping statements, self-love exercises, and more! The bonus chapter will help to create more peace of mind when feeling anxious.

The Anxiety Healer's Guide

THOUGHTS vs. FEELINGS

Guess whether the statement is a thought of a feeling
(place a check mark under the correct answer).

	Thought	Feeling
I am lonely.		
I am a failure.		
I am useless.		
I feel anxious.		
Nothing ever goes right.		
I am scared.		
Everything is falling apart.		
I am so angry.		
My life will never get better.		
I am so ashamed.		

The Anxiety Healer's Guide

EXAMPLE AUTOMATIC THOUGHTS CHECKLIST

Instructions: Place a check mark beside each automatic negative thought (ANT) that you have had in the pas or currently.

_____ I should be doing better in life.

_____ He/she doesn't understand me.

_____ I've let him/her down.

_____ I just can't enjoy things anymore.

_____ Why am I so weak?

_____ I always keep messing things up.

_____ My life's going nowhere.

_____ I can't handle it.

_____ I'm failing.

_____ It's too much for me.

_____ I don't have much of a future.

_____ Things are out of control.

_____ Something bad is sure to happen.

_____ There is something wrong with me.

Add your own automatic negative thoughts below:

....

....

....

....

....

The Anxiety Healer's Guide

SITUATION

IDENTIFY TWO AUTOMATIC NEGATIVE THOUGHTS (ANT)

1.

2.

Label the cognitive distortion.

What feelings are connected to these thoughts?

Feelings List

Accepting/Open
Calm
Centered
Content
Fulfilled
Patient
Peaceful
Present
Relaxed
Serene
Trusting

Alive/Joyful
Amazed
Awed
Blissful
Delighted
Eager
Ecstatic
Enchanted
Energized
Engaged
Enthusiastic
Excited
Free
Happy
Inspired
Invigorated
Lively
Passionate
Playful
Radiant
Refreshed
Rejuvenated
Renewed
Satisfied
Thrilled
Vibrant

Angry/Annoyed
Agitated
Aggravated
Bitter
Contemptuous
Cynical
Disdainful
Disgruntled
Disturbed
Edgy
Exasperated
Frustrated
Furious
Grouchy
Hostile
Impatient
Irritated
Irate
Moody
On edge
Outraged
Pissed
Resentful
Upset
Vindictive

Courageous/Powerful
Adventurous
Brave
Capable
Confident
Daring
Determined
Free
Grounded
Proud
Strong
Worthy
Valiant

Connected/Loving
Accepting
Affectionate
Caring
Compassionate
Empathetic
Fulfilled
Present
Safe
Warm
Worthy
Curious
Engaged
Exploring
Fascinated
Interested
Intrigued
Involved
Stimulated

Despairing/Sad
Anguish
Depressed
Despondent
Disappointed
Discouraged
Forlorn
Gloomy
Grief
Heartbroken
Hopeless
Lonely
Longing
Melancholic
Sorrowful
Teary
Unhappy
Upset
Weary
Yearning

Feelings List

Disconnected/ Numb
Aloof
Bored
Confused
Distant
Empty
Indifferent
Isolated
Lethargic
Listless
Removed
Resistant
Shut down
Uneasy
Withdrawn

Embarrassed/ Shameful
Ashamed
Humiliated
Inhibited
Mortified
Self-conscious
Useless
Weak
Worthless

Fearful
Afraid
Anxious
Apprehensive
Frightened
Hesitant
Nervous
Panicked
Paralyzed
Scared
Terrified
Worried

Fragile
Helpless
Sensitive

Grateful
Appreciative
Blessed
Delighted
Fortunate
Graceful
Humbled
Lucky
Moved
Thankful
Touched

Guilty
Regretful
Remorseful
Sorry

Hopeful
Encouraged
Expectant
Optimistic
Trusting

Powerless
Impotent
Incapable
Resigned
Trapped
Victimized

Tender
Calm
Caring
Loving
Reflective
Self-loving
Serene
Vulnerable
Warm

Stressed/Tense
Anxious
Burned out
Cranky
Depleted
Edgy
Exhausted
Frazzled
Overwhelmed
Rattled
Rejecting
Restless
Shaken
Tight
Weary
Worn out

Unsettled/ Doubtful
Apprehensive
Concerned
Dissatisfied
Disturbed
Grouchy
Hesitant
Inhibited
Perplexed
Questioning
Rejecting
Reluctant
Shocked
Skeptical
Suspicious
Ungrounded
Unsure
Worried

Body Sensations

Achy	Gentle	Shaky
Airy	Hard	Shivery
Blocked	Heavy	Slow
Breathless	Hollow	Smooth
Bruised	Hot	Soft
Burning	Icy	Sore
Buzzy	Itchy	Spacey
Clammy	Jumpy	Spacious
Clenched	Knotted	Sparkly
Cold	Light	Stiff
Constricted	Loose	Still
Contained	Nauseated	Suffocated
Contracted	Numb	Sweaty
Dizzy	Painful	Tender
Drained	Pounding	Tense
Dull	Prickly	Throbbing
Electric	Pulsing	Tight
Empty	Queasy	Tingling
Expanded	Radiating	Trembly
Flowing	Relaxed	Twitchy
Fluid	Releasing	Vibrating
Fluttery	Rigid	Warm
Frozen	Sensitive	Wobbly
Full	Settled	Wooden

List of Healing Coping Statements

- · I am in the process of positive change.
- · I forgive myself and set myself free.
- · I accept myself and create peace in my mind and heart.
- · I rise above the thoughts that are trying to make me frightened.
- · I am willing to let go of tension, fear, and stress.
- · I have the power to make changes.
- · I am in the process of positive change.
- · I am safe in this moment.
- · I am loved and I am at peace.
- · I am healthy, whole, and complete.
- · I am safe in the universe.
- · I am open and willing to change.
- · I am in charge. I now take my own power back.
- · I am lovable and worth knowing.
- · I have the courage to make this a great day.
- · With each new breath, I inhale strength and exhale fear.
- · Everything I need comes to me at the right time.
- · It is safe for me to express my feelings.

5 Things You Love about Yourself

1.

2.

3.

4.

5.

Worry Time

SCHEDULING TIME TO WORRY

This is another mental ploy that is paradoxical in nature, simlar to the technique of accepting your worry. Instead of resisting your obsessions, you will choose periods during the day that you purposely devote to obsessing. See how peculiar that sounds, to instruct you to actually worry more! That's how you can recognize a paradoxical technique; it sounds wrong!

- Set aside two "worry times" of ten minutes each every day.

- Spend this entire time thinking only about your worries regarding one issue.

- Do not think about any positive alternatives, only the negative ones.

- And do not convince yourself that your worries are irrational.

- Attempt to become as anxious as possible while worrying.

- Continue to the end of each worry period, even if you run out of ideas and have to repeat the same worries over again.

- At the end of ten minutes, let go of those worries with some calming breaths, then return to other activities.

Worry Time

WORRY SCHEDULE

Print copies of this page to use for your daily "worry times"
and then rip the paper up once you're done and "throw the worries away."

Worry Time #1
My worries

Worry Time #2
My worries

Sleep Hygiene

1. **Set a schedule.**
   Make a sleep schedule; try to go to bed and wake up at the same time every day.

2. **Turn off electronics.**
   Avoid your phone, TV, and computer for at least thirty minutes before closing your eyes to fall asleep. Try something such as reading or listening to a sleep story on a meditation app such as Insight Timer or Calm.

3. **Don't force it.**
   If you haven't fallen asleep within twenty minutes, do some relaxing yoga poses or stretches, read a book, or listen to a meditation.

4. **Avoid caffeine, alcohol, and nicotine.**
   Caffeine can stay in your body for up to twelve hours, so try to avoid it as much as possible, even during the day. Remember that decaf also has caffeine in it!

5. **Use your bed only for sleeping and romance.**
   Your body will start to associate your bed with stimulating work activities if you do them from your bed. Try to keep the bed a place for only sleeping and intimate physical play with your partner.

6. **Don't nap during the day.**
   This will mess up your sleep cycle.

7. **Move your body.**
   Exercise and movement promote a healthy mind and body, which will help your sleeping habits. Avoid any strenuous exercise at least two hours before bed.

8. **Improve your sleep environment.**
   Sleep in an area that is quiet, comfortable, and dark. Try using an eye mask and eliminate as much noise as possible.

9. **Have a bedtime routine.**
   Make a calming routine part of your sleep hygiene. It could look like this:
   - 9:00 PM: take a hot bath or shower
   - 9:15 PM: brush teeth
   - 9:20 PM: turn on essential oil diffuser
   - 9:30 PM: read a book/journal
   - 9:45 PM: turn off lights and listen to sleep meditation/sleep story or do breathwork

Bedtime Routine Worksheet

Time	Activity	Calming Tools	Completed

Belly Breathing

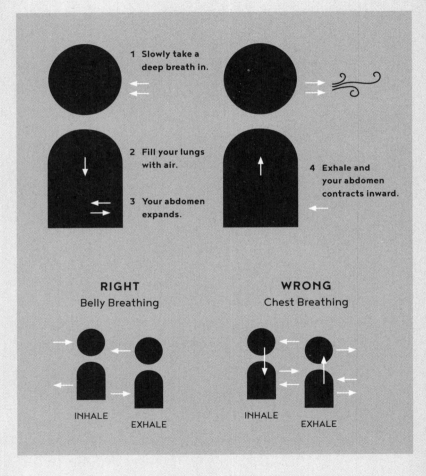

1 Slowly take a deep breath in.

2 Fill your lungs with air.

3 Your abdomen expands.

4 Exhale and your abdomen contracts inward.

RIGHT
Belly Breathing

INHALE

EXHALE

WRONG
Chest Breathing

INHALE

EXHALE

Belly Breathing Benefits

- Helps you relax by lowering the harmful effects of the stress hormone cortisol on your body
- Lowers your heart rate and blood pressure
- Helps you cope with the symptoms of anxiety
- Improves your core muscle stability
- Improves your body's ability to tolerate intense exercise
- Lowers your chances of injuring or wearing out your muscles
- Slows your rate of breathing so that it expends less energy

Trace Your Fingers to Calm Your Breath

Use this picture of your own hand to complete this exercise.

Spread your hand and stretch your fingers out like a star. You can choose your left hand or your right hand. Pretend the pointer finger of your other hand is a pencil and imagine you are going to trace around the outline of your hand and fingers.

INHALE through your **NOSE** as you trace upward.

PAUSE at the top of each finger.

EXHALE through your **MOUTH** as you trace downward.

PAUSE at the bottom.

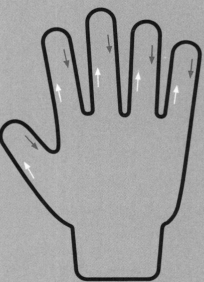

How does your body feel now?

Rewire Your Brain

MY TOP FIVE ANXIETY-HEALING COPING STATEMENTS

1.

2.

3.

4.

5.

Put these statements in your alerts every hour so you can
be reminded that YOU GOT THIS!

Stop Sign Technique

Intrusive thoughts can disrupt your life and become a major source of anxiety. This visualization exercise helps stop those unwanted thoughts in their tracks.

STOP

Imagine a stop sign when you have an unwanted anxious thought.

STEP 1:

Visualize a big red stop sign on an empty street with a clear blue sky overhead.

STEP 2:

Focus on the stop sign and repeat the word "stop."

STEP 3:

Observe and acknowledge the intrusive thought(s). Say to yourself, "I know anxiety is trying to make me believe that I'm in danger right now, but thoughts are *just thoughts* . . . thoughts do not have power."

Coloring Pages

ANXIETY . . .

. . . WARRIOR

I AM
IN CONTROL

THOUGHTS ARE
NOT FACTS

YOU. GOT. THIS.

I HAVE POWER OVER MY ANXIETY

ANXIETY . . .

DOES NOT
DEFINE ME

BREATHE

I AM SAFE

JUST LIKE BEFORE, I WILL SURVIVE THIS SITUATION

Distraction Games

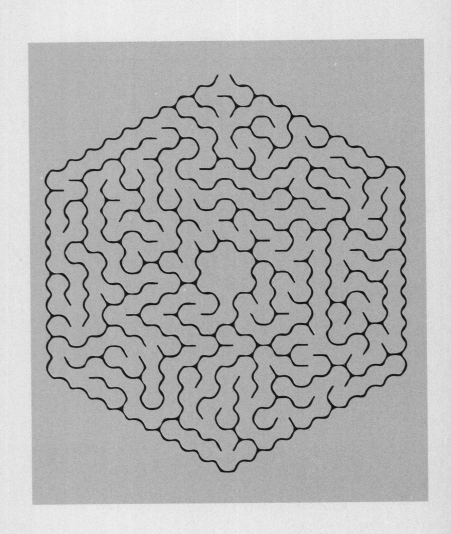

THE ANXIETY HEALER'S GUIDE

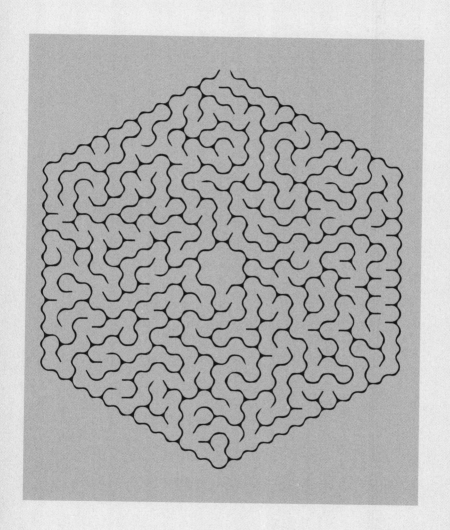

Connect the Dots

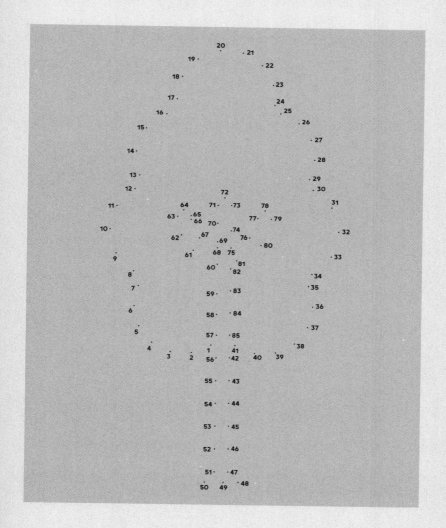

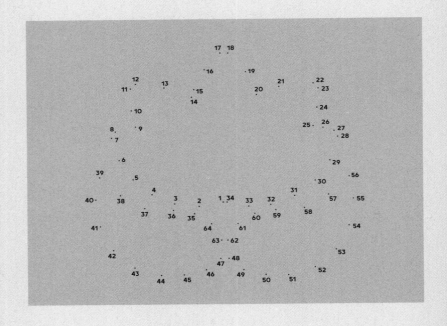

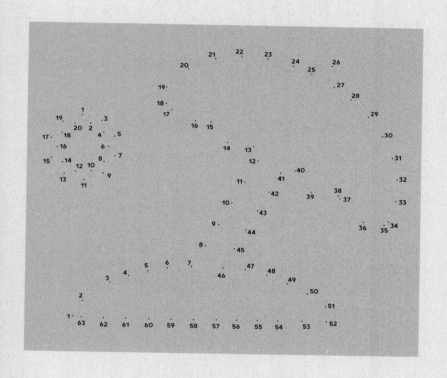

Acknowledgments

I would like to thank my mom and dad for always supporting my love of helping others and sacrificing their time and energy so that I could follow my passion as a healer. You both deserve so much appreciation and credit. Without you, I would not be who I am today.

So much love to my sister, Amy, who has been a huge part of my healing journey and provided me with unconditional loving support when I found it hard to believe that things could get better. You are one of the most important "pieces" of my healing tool kit. Also, a big thanks to my brother-in-law, Jonny, who is a true brother to me and chose not to give up on me in my darkest moments. You both gave me the most healing tools of them all—my niece, Emiliana, and my godson, Paolo. Thank you both for welcoming me into your family as if it were my own and showing me the importance of true family values.

Special acknowledgment goes to the incredible Ronnie Alvarado, my editor at Simon Element, who believed in this project and believed in the writer I never knew I wanted to be. She had a vision of what this book could be from the very beginning and saw the importance of spreading holistic healing to the rest of the world. I will be forever thankful.

Thank you to the entire publishing team at Simon & Schuster, including Jessica Preeg, Nan Rittenhouse, Emily Frick, Benjamin Holmes, Laura Flavin, Molly Pieper, and Kate Davids.

Special thanks to my best friend and writer Dorothy Simone (Cascerceri), who has been with me on my healing journey since 1995. Thank you for your wisdom and advice as a seasoned writer and for always supporting me in my personal and professional journey.

To all the academic researchers, clinicians, and theorists whose ideas and work make up the science of the book, including Dr. Nicole LePera, Dr. Dan Siegel, Louis Hay, Gary Craig, Albert Ellis, Aaron Beck, and the many others referenced throughout the text.

Finally, a special acknowledgment goes to all the amazing healers who have followed my work as the Anxiety Healer on Instagram. I am inspired by your courage to share your deepest fears and emotions on my page in order to help other healers feel less alone in their pain and suffering. You have created an incredibly safe space for those who struggle with anxiety and work so hard to help end the stigma of mental health. I am in awe of you every day. Thank you for creating a healing space for me and others around the world.

Bibliography

"Aromatherapy: Do Essential Oils Really Work?" Johns Hopkins University, accessed September 20, 2020. https://www.hopkinsmedicine.org/health/wellness-and-prevention/aromatherapy-do-essential-oils-really-work.

Batchu, Bala Kishore. "Neuro-Science Behind Visualization." International Coach Academy, December 3, 2013. https://coachcampus.com/coach-portfolios/research-papers/bala-kishore-batchu-neuro-science-behind-visualization/3.

Breit, Sigrid, et al. "Vagus Nerve as Modulator of the Brain-Gut Axis in Psychiatric and Inflammatory Disorders." *Frontiers in Psychiatry* 9 (March 2018): 44.

Cho, Eun Hee, et al. "The Effects of Aromatherapy on Intensive Care Unit Patients' Stress and Sleep Quality: A Nonrandomized Controlled Trial." *Evidence-Based Complementary and Alternative Medicine* 2017 (December 2017): 2856592. doi:10.1155/2017/2856592.

Clark, D., and A. Beck. *The Anxiety and Worry Workbook: The Cognitive Behavioral Solution.* New York: Guilford Press, 2012.

"Cognitive Model." Beck Institute: Cognitive Behavioral Therapy, accessed November 21, 2020. https://beckinstitute.org/cognitive-model/.

Cully, J. A., and A. L. Teten. "A Therapist's Guide to Brief Cognitive Behavioral Therapy." Houston: Department of Veterans Affairs, South Central MIRECC, 2008. https://depts.washington.edu/dbpeds/therapists_guide_to_brief_cbtmanual.pdf.

Eddins, Rachel, MEd. "Grounding Techniques & Self Soothing for Emotional Regulation." Eddison Counseling, April 1, 2020. https://eddinscounseling.com/grounding-techniques-self-soothing-emotional-regulation/.

"EFT Tapping." Healthline, accessed September 22, 2020. https://www.healthline.com/health/eft-tapping.

Eisler, Melissa. "Nadi Shodhana: How to Practice Alternate Nostril Breathing." Chopra, November 15, 2015. https://chopra.com/articles/nadi-shodhana-how-to-practice-alternate-nostril-breathing.

Gawain, Shakti. *Creative Visualization: Use the Power of Your Imagination to Create What You Want in Your Life*. Novato, CA: Nataraj Publishing, 2002.

"Grounding Techniques: Step-by-Step Guide and Methods." Medical News Today, March 31, 2020. https://www.medicalnewstoday.com/articles/grounding-techniques#methods.

Harandi, T. F., M. M. Taghinasab, and T. D. Nayeri. "The Correlation of Social Support with Mental Health: A Meta-analysis." *Electronic Physician* 9, no. 9 (September 2017): 5212–22. doi:10.19082/5212.

Hay, Louise. *Experience Your Good Now!: Learning to Use Affirmations*. Carlsbad, CA: Hay House, 2010.

———. "What Is Mirror Work?" Accessed November 15, 2020. https://www.louisehay.com/what-is-mirror-work/.

"How to Choose the Best Aromatherapy Oil." My Chinese Recipes, February 27, 2020. https://www.mychineserecipes.com/how-to-choose-the-best-aromatherapy-oil/.

Jaehnig, Jon. "Free Association: What Is It, and How Does It Work?" Betterhelp, November 10, 2020. https://www.betterhelp.com/advice/psychologists/free-association-what-is-it-and-how-does-it-work/.

Jasemi, M., S. Aazami, and R. E. Zabihi. "The Effects of Music Therapy on Anxiety and Depression of Cancer Patients." *Indian Journal of Palliative Care* 22, no. 4 (October–December 2016): 455–58. doi: 10.4103/0973-1075.191823.

Jerath, Ravinder, et al. "Self-Regulation of Breathing as a Primary Treatment for Anxiety." *Applied Psychophysiology and Biofeedback* 40, no. 2 (June 2015): 107–15. doi: 10.1007/s10484-015-9279-8.

Jungmann, M., et al. "Effects of Cold Stimulation on Cardiac-Vagal Activation in Healthy Participants: Randomized Controlled Trial." *JMIR Formative Research* 2, no. 2 (October 2018): e10257. doi:10.2196/10257.

Kim, Jung T., et al. "Evaluation of Aromatherapy in Treating Postoperative Pain: Pilot Study." *Pain Practice* 6, no. 4 (November 2006): 273–77.

Kirchell, Sally. "10 Benefits of Starting Your Day with Positive Affirmations." Elephant Journal, November 28, 2018. https://www.elephant journal.com/2018/11/10-benefits-of-starting-your-day-with-positive -affirmations-2/.

"Learn Bhastrika Pranayama (Bellows Breath)." Yoga International. https:// yogainternational.com/article/view/learn-bhastrika-pranayama-bellows -breath.

LePera, Nicole. *How to Do the Work: Recognize Your Patterns, Heal from Your Past, and Create Your Self.* London: Orion Spring, 2021.

———. Vagus Nerve: A Path to Healing." Holistic Psychologist, September 9, 2018. https://yourholisticpsychologist.com/vagus_nerve_a_path-to-healing/.

Lizarraga-Valderrama, Lorena R. "Effects of Essential Oils on Central Nervous System: Focus on Mental Health." *Psychotherapy Research* 35, no. 2 (February 2021): 657–79.

Luberto, C. M., et al. "A Perspective on the Similarities and Differences Between Mindfulness and Relaxation." *Global Advances in Health and Medicine* 9 (January 2020): 1–13. doi: 10.1177/2164956120905597.

Marksberry, Kellie. "Take a Deep Breath." American Institute of Stress, August 10, 2012. https://www.stress.org/take-a-deep-breath.

McCorry, Laurie Kelly. "Physiology of the Autonomic Nervous System." *American Journal of Pharmaceutical Education* 71, no. 4 (August 2007): 78. doi:10.5688/aj710478.

Mizrahi, Maya C., et al. "Effects of Guided Imagery with Relaxation Training on Anxiety and Quality of Life Among Patients with Inflammatory Bowel Disease." *Psychology & Health* 27, no. 12 (May 2012): 1463–79. doi:10.1080 /08870446.2012.691169.

Monet, Michelle. "Neuroplasticity Is Mind Boggling Science." Invincible Illness, September 4, 2019. https://medium.com/invisible-illness/neuroplasti city-is-mind-boggling-science-29a215e44096.

Mooventhan, A., and L. Nivethitha. "Scientific Evidence-Based Effects of Hydrotherapy on Various Systems of the Body." *North American Journal of Medical Sciences* 6, no. 5 (May 2014): 199–209. doi: 10.4103/1947-2714.132935.

"Panic Attacks." University of Pennsylvania, December 11, 2020. https://www.med.upenn.edu/ctsa/panic_symptoms.html.

"Relaxation Techniques for Health." National Center for Complementary and Integrative Health, May 10, 2018. https://nccih.nih.gov/health/stress/relaxation.htm.

Scholey, A., et al. "Chewing Gum Alleviates Negative Mood and Reduces Cortisol During Acute Laboratory Psychological Stress." *Physiology & Behavior* 97, nos. 3–4 (June 2009): 304–12. doi: 10.1016/j.physbeh.2009.02.028.

Smith, J. M., and L. B. Alloy. "A Roadmap to Rumination: A Review of the Definition, Assessment, and Conceptualization of this Multifaceted Construct." *Clinical Psychology Review* 29, no. 2 (March 2009): 116–28. doi:10.1016/j.cpr.2008.10.003.

"Stress Effects on the Body." American Psychological Association, November 1, 2018. https://www.apa.org/topics/stress/body.

"Stressing Out? S.T.O.P." Mindful, May 29, 2013. https://www.mindful.org/stressing-out-stop.

Toda, M., K. Morimoto, S. Nagasawa, and K. Kitamura. "Change in Salivary Physiological Stress Markers by Spa Bathing." *Biomedical Research* 27, no. 1 (February 2006): 11–14. doi: 10.2220/biomedres.27.11.

Tseng, J., and J. Poppenk. "Brain Meta-State Transitions Demarcate Thoughts Across Task Contexts Exposing the Mental Noise of Trait Neuroticism." *Nature Communications* 11 (July 2020): 3480. https://doi.org/10.1038/s41467-020-17255-9.

"Understanding the Stress Response." Harvard Medical School, July 6, 2020. https://www.health.harvard.edu/staying-healthy/understanding-the-stress-response.

"Visualization and Guided Imagery Techniques for Stress Reduction." Mentalhealth.net. https://www.mentalhelp.net/stress/visualization-and-guided-imagery-techniques-for-stress-reduction/.

Weil, Andrew. "Three Breathing Exercises and Techniques." DrWeil.com, May 2016. https://www.drweil.com/health-wellness/body-mind-spirit/stress-anxiety/breathing-three-exercises/.

Wells, Rachel. "5 Ways to Stop Panic in Its Tracks." Happify Daily, accessed January 18, 2021. https://www.happify.com/hd/5-ways-to-stop-panic-in-its-tracks/.

"What Is Mindfulness?" *Greater Good Magazine*, February 10, 2021. https://greatergood.berkeley.edu/topic/mindfulness/definition.

"What Is Tapping and How Can I Start Using It?" Tapping Solution, accessed September 12, 2020. https://www.thetappingsolution.com/what-is-eft-tapping/.

"What's the Difference Between a Panic Attack and an Anxiety Attack?" Healthline, September 30, 2019. https://www.healthline.com/health/panic-attack-vs-anxiety-attack.

Wong, Kristin. "Journaling Showdown: Writing vs. Typing." Lifehacker, March 5, 2017. https://lifehacker.com/journaling-showdown-writing-vs-typing-1792942629.

Index

brain
    creating catastrophic response to
        situations, xii–xiii
    EFT tapping and, 41, 42
    "fear-based," xxii
    nervous system and, xv–xvii, 4
    neuroplasticity, 51, 108–9
    rest and digest part of, 7
"Breath, The" relaxation script, 85–87
breathing techniques and breathwork. *See
    also* belly breathing
    alternate nostril breathing, 14, 15
    apps, 16–17
    bellows breathing (*bhastrika*), 11–12
    Blowing Out the Candles exercise, 16
    "Breath, The" relaxation script,
        85–87
    with body relaxation script, 84–85
    in example of anxiety-healing tool
        kit, 152
    4-7-8 breathing technique, 13, 15
    as grounding tool, 30, 31, 33
    in "Happy Place" relaxation script,
        88–90
    "Here and Now, The" relaxation
        script, 87–88
    journaling/schedules for, 18–19
    Lion's Breath, 6–7
    online searches about, 18
    recording in your journal, 18–19
    rectangle, 5, 6
    science of, 4, 6
    Star breathing exercise, 9–10
    tracing fingers to calm, 175
    two-minute calming meditation,
        38–39
    using your imagination to practice,
        15–16
    for visualization exercises, 110, 112
    Zen Word Breathing, 9
bubble wrap, 64
bus, grounding tools for when you are
    in a, 31
butterfly observation, xxiii
B vitamins, 66

C

calming exercises. *See* two-minute
    calming exercises
calming phrases, 94–95

calming technique cards, 64–65
candles, 77
cards from others, in self-soothing box, 77
car, grounding tools for when you are
    in a, 30
car, self-talk/affirmations in the, 96
catastrophizing, xxiv
categories, naming items in different, 26,
    135, 136–37
CBD oil, 65
CBT. *See* cognitive behavioral therapy
    (CBT)
chest pain, xiv
chewing gum, 65
childhood experiences/adversity, self-
    soothing and, 63
chills, xv
Chinese medicine, EFT tapping and, 42
choking, feeling of, xv
cognitive behavioral therapy (CBT), xxii,
    xxiv–xxvi
cognitive distortions, xxiv, xxviii–xxix, 164
cold towel, 65
cold water immersion hydrotherapy, 37
coloring books, 64
coloring pages, 179–88
connected/loving feelings, 165
Connect the Dots, 195–97
coping card, 30
coping statements
    in example of anxiety-healing tool
        kit, 153
    as grounding tool, 30
    "I" statements, 39
    list of healing, 168
    My Top Five Anxiety-Healing, 177
    as self-soothing tool, 65
cortisol, xvi, 4, 39
counting
    distraction technique, 25–26
    as grounding tool, 30, 32
courageous/powerful feelings, 165
crafting, 132
Craig, Gary, 41
creative visualization, 119–25
crystal (self-soothing object), 29

D

daily breathwork schedule, 19
daily mirror work, 104

dancing, 130
depersonalization, 22
derealization, 22, 36, 40
description game, two-minute, 36–37
despairing/sad feelings, 165
diaphragmatic (belly) breathing. *See* belly
     breathing
dietitians, 145
diffusers, essential oils in, 70, 71
digestive issues, ix
digital vision boards, 123–24
disconnected/numb feelings, 166
disqualifying the positive, xxviii
distraction apps, 73–74, 130–31
distraction games, 32, 134–35, 189–97
distraction techniques
     about, 129
     categories game, 136–37
     changing your environment, 129–30
     creating a list of happy things, 137
     entertaining yourself, 130–31
     in example of anxiety-healing tool
          kit, 155
     making a "best of" list, 135–36
     singing, 130
     walking, 136
     writing, 133–34
dive reflex, 38
DO (doctor of osteopathic medicine), 148
doctor, questions to ask a, 144
doctor's office
     grounding tools for when you are in
          a, 31–32
     self-talk/affirmations in, 95–96
     visiting your primary-care doctor,
          143–44
double-paned window technique, 119
dry mouth, xv
DSM-5, anxiety attacks in, 3

E

Eastern medicine, ix
eating, mindful, 145
EdD (doctor of education), 148
EFT tapping
     eight body tapping points, 45
     explained, 41–42
     how to practice, 42–43, 46
     karate chop (KC) point, 43, 44
     two-minute, 41–46

embarrassed/shameful feelings, 166
emotional awareness/intelligence,
     xx–xxii
Emotional Freedom Technique. *See* EFT
     tapping
emotional reasoning, xviii
emotions. *See* feelings
energy
     thoughts and, 119–20
     visualization goal and positive, 122
environment, changing your, 129–30
essential oils, 41
     application of, 68, 69
     aromatherapy with, 68, 70–71
     irritation or allergic reactions to, 69
     in self-soothing box, 77
     self-soothing with, 29, 65
     shopping for the right, 69–70
     that are known to help with moods
          and energy, 71
     that are known to relieve stress,
          68–69
everyday grounding, 32
exercise, 130
eye mask, 65

F

fainting, xiv
family/family events
     grounding tools when you are with,
          31
     self-talk/affirmations at, 97
fear and fearful feelings, xii–xiii, 107,
     166
feather (self-soothing object), 29
feelings
     automatic negative thoughts and,
          164
     distinguishing thoughts from, 162
     emotional awareness/intelligence,
          xx–xxi
     feeling your, in "The Breath"
          relaxation script, 86
     list of different types of, 165–66
     matching music to your, 47–49
     naming your, xx
feelings journal, xxii
fidget spinner, 65, 76, 152
fight-or-flight response, xv–xvi
five senses grounding technique, 23–24

restaurants
  grounding tools for when you are
    in, 31
  self-talk/affirmations in, 95
robiola, 65
rock (self-soothing object), 29
Rubik's Cube, 29, 67

S

sad/despairing feelings, 165
"safe," feeling with others, 132
"Safe Place, The" visualization script,
  115–17
sand, bag of, 67
schedule(ing)
  bedtime, 172
  breathwork, 19
  for journaling, 52
  for Lion's Breath, 7
  mirror work, 104–5
  sleep, 172
  worry, 171
scratch-and-sniff stickers, 67
scripts
  anxiety-healing grounding, 26–28
  used for guided meditations, 83–91
  visualization, 109–18, 124–25
see, identifying and naming what you,
  23, 40, 87
self-advocacy
  finding the right therapist, 146
  mindful eating, 145
  self-reflection exercise, 150
  support system and, 149
  when visiting your primary-care
    doctor, 143–44
self-awareness, xvii
self-love, 169
self-reflective journal prompts, 53–54
self-soothing tools
  body scan, 57–60
  effect on nervous system, 63
  in example of anxiety-healing tool
    kit, 152
  goal of, 64
  journaling and journal prompts, 50–55
  keyword phrases to search online for,
    78
  making your own self-soothing box,
    76–78

music, 47–50
objects, 28–29, 30, 76–77
portable items, 64–67
progressive muscle relaxation (PMR)
  technique, 56–57
self-talk, 83–105
  affirmations, 92–95, 101–2
  automatic negative thoughts,
    163–64
  "Body Relaxation" script, 84–85
  to break the negativity loop, 92–99
  "Breath, The" relaxation script,
    85–87
  in cars, 96
  changing negative, 99–100
  in doctor's offices, 95–96
  at family events, 97
  in grocery stores, 98
  "Happy Place" relaxation script,
    88–90
  "Here and Now, The" relaxation
    script, 87–88
  mirror work with, 102–5
  "Morning Meditation," 90–91
  at nighttime, 98–99
  in restaurants, 95–96
  at social events, 96–97
  at work, 97–98
senses
  describing your surroundings, 37
  focus on, in "The Here and Now"
    relaxation script, 87–88
  self-soothing items for, 77
  two-minute grounding tool using
    your five, 40–41
  using in two-minute description
    game, 36
seven key questions activity, 24–25
shaking, xiv
shameful/embarrassed feelings, 166
shift breathing necklace, 67
shortness of breath, xiii, xiv, 3, 4
"should" statements, xxviii
shower(ing), cold-water immersion
  hydrotherapy in, 37–38
Silly Putty, 67, 76
singing, as distraction technique, 130
sleep and sleep hygiene
  affirmations at bedtime and, 98–99
  bedtime routine worksheet, 173

video games, 130, 132
videos, in example of anxiety-healing tool kit, 154
vision board, 122–24
visualization, 107–27
    about a happy memory, 118
    about your future, 125–27
    creative, 119–25
    double-paned window, 119
    in example of anxiety-healing tool kit, 153
    explained, 107
    guided imagery, 107–8
    introduction script for, 109–12
    "Pond, The" script, 112–13
    recording scripts, 109
    rewiring your brain and, 108–9
    "Safe Place, The" script, 115–17
    stop sign technique, 178
    "White Sandy Beach, The" visualization script, 113–15
vitamins and supplements, 65–66

W

walks/walking, 130, 136
water
    cold, as grounding tool, 30, 31, 32
    in self-soothing box, 76
    two-minute hydrotherapy, 37–38
water intake, 67
weekly breathwork schedule, 19
weighted blanket, 67
"what if" thoughts and questions, xxviii, 99
"White Sandy Beach, The" visualization script, 113–15
word games, 67
work, self-talk/affirmations at, 97–98
worry. *See also* anxiety/anxiety disorder
    scheduling a time for, 170
    writing down and then ripping up, 171
worry stone, 67
writing. *See also* journal(ing)
    about your future self, 126
    affirmations, 93–94

Y

yoga, 131

Z

Zen Word Breathing, 9

About the Author

Alison Seponara, MS, LPC, is a licensed psychotherapist and anxiety healer in Philadelphia. Alison specializes in cognitive behavioral therapy and mindfulness-based positive psychology with individuals who struggle with anxiety disorders. Known as "The Anxiety Healer" on Instagram, Alison has created a mental health awareness brand that helps other anxiety sufferers feel less alone in their journey toward healing. Alison refers to community members as "healers" as a way to create more unity and inclusivity among her followers. Alison uses her social media platforms to speak openly and honestly about her own anxiety struggles, while offering compassion and empathy to those who can relate. Alison is dedicated to ending the stigma of mental health by offering a safe space for those around the world to find a supportive community free of judgment and bias.

Alison is also the host of *The Anxiety Chicks*, a podcast in which she uses her expertise as a therapist and her own life experience to educate listeners on anxiety disorders, mind/body connection, panic attacks, gut health, holistic remedies, and, most important, how to keep it real when it comes to talking about mental health. Alison is the founder of the Anxiety Healing School, an online curriculum with multiple healing courses that help students learn how to combat intrusive thoughts, face fears, and rewire the anxious brain.